Sylvanus Dryden Phelps

Rest Days in a Journey to Bible Lands

And Other Journeys Abroad - Sermons Preached in the Four Quarters of the Globe

Sylvanus Dryden Phelps

Rest Days in a Journey to Bible Lands
And Other Journeys Abroad - Sermons Preached in the Four Quarters of the Globe

ISBN/EAN: 9783337127893

Printed in Europe, USA, Canada, Australia, Japan

Cover: Foto ©Lupo / pixelio.de

More available books at **www.hansebooks.com**

REST DAYS

IN A

Journey to Bible Lands

AND OTHER JOURNEYS ABROAD

SERMONS

PREACHED IN THE FOUR QUARTERS OF THE GLOBE

By S. DRYDEN PHELPS, D.D.

WITH PREFATORY NOTES AND ILLUSTRATIONS

New York
WARD & DRUMMOND 116 NASSAU STREET
Christian Secretary Offices
HARTFORD   NEW HAVEN
336 Asylum St.   44 High St.
1887

PREFACE.

SABBATHS abroad are true Rest Days to Christian travelers. They are full of pleasant memories. One may count it as a unique experience to have preached in such widely separated localities, and this book is to me a precious memorial of those occasions and of the dear friends who were with me, several of whom are now enjoying the Rest Days of Heaven. While repeating to my congregation the sermons preached during my first tour, prefacing them with the circumstances under which they were spoken, it was suggested that they be published. To give something more of size to the volume, as well as interest, the preliminary notes have been included; and then, to add still more of matter and variety, the fancy took me to append to the discourses original hymns or verses, bearing on the same subjects, and to insert also some illustrations of places or objects at or near where the sermons were delivered. Great delay in bringing out the book, for lack of leisure for it, has allowed me to add three sermons preached during subsequent tours to Europe. The work is a sort of appendix to my "Holy Land, with Glimpses of Egypt and Europe," which was so favorably received as to reach a ninth edition.

S. D. P.

NEW HAVEN, DEC., 1886.

CONTENTS.

	PAGE
INTRODUCTION	5
A PASTOR'S JOURNEY AND ABSENCE FROM HIS FLOCK	7

Prefatory Notes precede each Sermon, giving the circumstances under which it was preached.

SERMON I.—*ATLANTIC OCEAN.*
SOJOURNING AND ITS PERILS - - - - 17
    1 PETER I. 17.—Pass the time of your sojourning here in fear.
    Hymn: The Beacon Light - - - - - - - 31
    Illustration: Entrance to the Harbor of St. Johns - - 33

SERMON II.—*DUBLIN, IRELAND.*
PILATE'S QUESTION—OURS - - - - - 39
    MATTHEW XXVII. 22.—What shall I do then with Jesus which is called Christ?
    Hymn: What Shall I Do with Jesus? - - - - - 56

SERMON III.—*MEDITERRANEAN SEA.*
OUR GREAT REFUGE - - - - - - 65
    ROMANS VIII. 31.—If God be for us, who can be against us?
    Hymn: Hymn of Trust - - - - - - - 82
    Illustration: St. Paul's Bay - - - - - - 60

SERMON IV.—*RIVER NILE, EGYPT.*
THE TEARLESS LAND - - - - - - 91
    REVELATION XXI. 4.—And God shall wipe away all tears from their eyes.
    Hymn: No Tears in Heaven - - - - - - 112
    Illustration: Pyramids and Sphinx - - - - - 86

SERMON V.—*MT. ZION, JERUSALEM.*

CHRIST ALONE - - - - - - 123
   ISAIAH LXIII. 3.—I have trodden the wine-press alone.
   Hymn: Gethsemane - - - - - - - 145
   Illustration: Jerusalem from the Northeast - - - 116
   Illustration: Olive-Trees in Gethsemane - - - - 147

SERMON VI.—*NEW HAVEN, CONN.*

THE LORD OUR HOME - - - - - 153
   PSALM XC 1.—Lord, thou hast been our dwelling place in all generations.
   Hymn: The Heart's Home . - - - - - 169
   Illustration: Interior View of the Church - - - 171

SERMON VII —*EDINBURGH.*

OPPOSITE SIDES OF THE PILLAR OF CLOUD AND
   FIRE - - - - - - - . 177
   EXODUS XIV. 20.—It came between the camp of the Egyptians and the camp of Israel; and it was a cloud and darkness to them, but it gave light by night to these.
   Hymn: The Pillar of Cloud and Fire - - - - 195
   Illustration: West Side of St. Giles's - - - - 197

SERMON VIII.—*ATLANTIC OCEAN.*

THE CALL AND THE RESPONSE - - - 203
   PSALM XLII. 7.—Deep calleth unto deep.
   Lines: A Memorial - - - - - - - 217
   Illustration: White Star Steamer Adriatic - - - 219

SERMON IX.—*AT SEA.*

CHRIST'S WORK FOR THE HUMAN RACE - 225
   JOHN I. 9.—That was the true light, which lighteth every man that cometh into the world.

INTRODUCTION.

LONG had it been my desire to make the journey out of which this book has grown. The Lands of the Bible had for me, from my earliest study of the Sacred Volume, an indescribable charm. Their mountains and valleys, their lakes and rivers, their cities and villages, their thoroughfares and pathways, and most of all, the historic, hallowed and tender associations connected with them, made them in my mind memorable and dear above all other localities on earth. To look upon them with my own eyes, to view objects that such other eyes had seen, to tread where such other feet had trod, and to actually visit places where the most wonderful and significant events in our world's history have occurred, were a golden dream whose realization might indeed be a marked epoch in one's life.

At length the time for the journey came. It was taken midway of a pleasant and prosperous pastorate of twenty-eight years with the Church where I was ordained. It was after an unprecedented religious awakening and interest among that people, which had continued for more than two years. My dear flock, aware of my need of rest and recreation, very kindly acceded to my request for time to visit Europe and the East, and most generously provided for its necessities. They gave me such leave of absence as I wanted, continued my salary as pastor, also took upon them the supply of the pulpit, and at a pleasant gathering just before my departure, presented to me a liberal purse. All they asked for these tokens of their noble kindness and affection was a monthly letter with some account of my travels.

Arrangements being completed, the Sabbath before I was to sail had come. It was a beautiful day in June. The audience-room of the Church was filled to repletion. All the services were adapted to the occasion. The hymns preceding and following the discourse were—"My days are gliding swiftly by," and "When shall we all meet again?" The Scriptures read were Psalm cxxii. and Philippians ii. The theme and text are here given, with some selections from the sermon, which was not a full manuscript.

A PASTOR'S JOURNEY AND ABSENCE FROM HIS FLOCK.

Acts xx. 22.—And now, behold, I go...unto Jerusalem, not knowing the things that shall befall me there.

Rom i. 10.—Making request, if by any means now at length I might have a prosperous journey by the will of God to come unto you.

Phil. ii. 12, 13.—Wherefore, my beloved, as ye have always, not as in my presence only, but now much more in my absence, work out your own salvation with fear and trembling. For it is God which worketh in you both to will and to do of his good pleasure.

When a person goes from home, to be away for any considerable time, three things are likely to absorb his attention. The farthest limit or chief spot of his journey rises prominently before him; then he considers his outward and homeward wanderings or travels; and at the same time his thoughts cling with a deep and sacred interest to those whom he leaves at home. These three things are contained in my text.

Now, after having cherished the desire so long, and thought and dreamed of it so much, am I really to have my feet stand within thy gates, O Jerusalem? Shall I see and climb the mountains that are around about the Holy City? Shall I visit the places where the prophets lived? and above all where Jesus walked and taught and died? Shall I go to Olivet, Gethsemane, Bethany, Bethlehem, the Jordan, the Sea of Galilee, Nazareth, and Jacob's Well? Shall I visit battle-fields where Joshua led the hosts to victory, where the sun stood still upon Gibeon and the moon in the vale of Ajalon? and places where Abram dwelt when he came from Ur of the Chaldees? I hope on my way to Palestine to visit the more ancient country and antiquities of Egypt; the land where the Pharaohs reigned; where Moses was cradled and wrought miracles; places and scenes of the cruel bondage, and those wonderful monuments, the Pyramids. Possibly I may go awhile in the track of the released Israelites, as they crossed the Red Sea, and entered the desert and journeyed by the wells and palms of Elim, and the sacred mountains of Sinai. To reach these distant localities I purpose to go first to England and various countries of Europe. I had hoped to make this journey before now, and should probably have gone a year earlier, but for the precious and wonderful religious interest God in His rich mercy has permitted us to enjoy. It is just three years this month since the gracious work commenced, and has continued with remarkable power and results, while the Spirit's influence still lingers with us. How could I go under such circumstances? How could I leave the dear converts and the church? But now, having had some experience, they will I trust remain stedfast.

It is not mere idle curiosity or disposition to rove abroad that induces the journey. There is a pleasure, and I enjoy it greatly, in visiting scenes and objects in nature and art, beautiful and sublime, and of which no adequate idea can be gained but by travel and personal inspection.

One purpose of the tour is change and rest, and the hope of mental and physical invigoration. I do not go as an invalid. I am not suffering from any disease. Still, after more than fourteen years of service in the ministry in one place, it is not strange that there should be some feeling of exhaustion. Mental cares and spiritual anxieties, with a too small allowance of physical exercise, after awhile wear and weigh upon one with a pressure that cannot well be described. Rest, travel, recreation—getting away on a sea-voyage perhaps, into new scenes of interest and grandeur—away from pressing responsibilities in a measure—having the mind diverted, interested, and the body exercised by travel and refreshed by an atmosphere to which it is unaccustomed; this is what is needed—this, if anything, will bring a rejuvenation to body and mind, both grateful and inspiring. Some of our best ministers, who have early broken down and gone to their graves, had they taken rest and travel, might have had their lives and usefulness prolonged.

Another prominent object of my contemplated journey is improvement in knowledge and experience. Who is sufficient for these things?—the things of the Christian ministry—said Paul. No calling has greater demands, or more use for all the talents and acquirements one may possess. Ministers have to deal with men—with human minds and consciences in all their conditions and phases. And there is no way to study men so well as to mingle with them and see them as they appear in different nations and degrees of civilization.

The Bible is the minister's great text-book. Many of its truths are modified or explained by local allusions, and there is no way to get this knowledge so well as by visiting and inspecting the sacred places of the Bible. We are often impressed as powerfully and beneficially through our sympathies and feelings as through our intellects. Let a man go to a battle-field where the dearest rights of man were contended for, and he will learn the better to appreciate his civil blessings. So let one visit Gethsemane or Calvary, and he will have impressions that no sermon could produce. His heart would be made better and be brought into deeper sympathy with the great truths associated with such localities. I would not go if I did not believe it would be better for my work as a minister, and better for you at length, in my future ministrations, if the Lord shall permit them longer here. So much for the purpose and objects of the journey.

In regard to the tour itself, I desire as the Apostle did that I may have a prosperous journey by the will of God *to come to you.* I shall no doubt be more anxious to come back than I am to go out. It is one of the severest trials I have ever experienced to tear myself away from this dear people and these loving hearts! But I cannot speak of this. "And now, behold, I go unto Jerusalem, not knowing what shall befall me there." Every considerable journey has its perils. We know not what is before us. The ocean, the land, the civilized and the barbaric country, all have their dangers. And where can we go or stay, at home or abroad, on the wave or the shore, that we are not more or less exposed to perils—to sickness, to calamity, to death.

He who goes abroad, and there to be ill and to die, might not have been exempt at home. Disaster may come here as well as there. To the Christian, wherever he may be, God is near, and Heaven is as easily reached from one point as from another.

I go in hope of the Divine blessing. God is our refuge. Under the shadow of His wings we rest. He holds the winds and the waves. He can turn the hearts of men. It is blessed to trust in Him, and cast every care on Him who careth for us. So I shall go with a cheerful heart, committing my ways to the Lord who has promised to direct my steps.

But "to come to you," to see your faces again, to hear your voices, to press your hands in which loving heart-beats are felt—this will be a constant hope and inspiration. The lines have fallen to me in pleasant places. Rare is it, I think, that a pastor has such a people—so kind, so affectionate, so generous, so disposed to overlook his faults, so anxious to render him tokens of their regard and favor. Your liberal arrangements for my journey have overwhelmed me with a sense of your affection, and excited grateful emotions beyond the power of language to express. My prayer is and shall be that God may reward you, dear brethren and friends, with His richest blessings. I may see many persons and faces, but none will be so pleasant as yours. I may enter many churches and grand cathedrals, but no sanctuary will have such attractions as this. May our Heavenly Father spare us to meet again!

Let me now, in closing, speak a little of what I

feel in regard to your welfare in my absence. This is a matter of deep solicitude on my part. Your spiritual prosperity will give me the highest joy; or, if it be otherwise, the deepest sadness. With you, as individuals, as a church and congregation, the responsibility mainly lies. If you hold on, united and faithful in all well-doing, God will bless and keep you. There must be resolution, activity, and self-denial for the sake of the cause. Each must fill his place. Paul said the Philippians in his absence were more obedient than in his presence. So may it be here. Work out your own salvation each with a keen sense of personal responsibility, and an implicit reliance on the Spirit and grace of God.

Thus shall the church continue to prosper, the congregations shall be kept full, and if God shall permit us to meet here again I shall find things on my return as well as if not better than I leave them.

We may not, very likely we shall not, all meet on earth again. It becomes us to be ready at all times for the coming of the Son of man. Let the aged pilgrims, those midway along the course, and the young converts, all, be true and faithful. Let this be your spiritual home. Be loyal to Christ and the church. Be in your place whoever may be in the pulpit.

Dear friends, who have not yet embraced the gospel, it gives me pain to leave you unconverted. If I should never address you again, let my last lingering word be an invitation to come to Christ.

SERMON I.

SOJOURNING AND ITS PERILS.

Atlantic Ocean.

PREFATORY NOTES.

JUST before taking passage at New York for Liverpool on the Inman Steamship City of Washington, it was learned that the Edinburgh had been partially wrecked by running upon an iceberg in the fog near Newfoundland, but by great exertion she had been got with safety into the harbor of St. Johns, and that our steamer was to stop there and receive her passengers. Of these were Mrs. Annie M. Douglas, a member of my church in New Haven, with her little son and a sister. It happened now, as we could not leave on the same vessel, as had been desired, that we should meet on the way and cross the ocean together.

After we left St. Johns with this large accession to our ship the topic of conversation and inquiry for a time was the disaster to the Edinburgh, with thrilling accounts of the collision, and the excitements and perils of the hour. Among the narrators of the scene were Mr. E. P. Hammond, then a theological student, now the distinguished revivalist, and Hon. A. H. Laflin of New York State, since a member of Congress, and late Naval Officer at New York. So dense was the fog that the iceberg was not seen till they were right upon it. Higher than the masts of the ship it rose, a truly magnificent object, but they only caught a glimpse of it, and were congratulating themselves on their escape, when they found to their dismay that the steamer was sinking. A rush was made for the boats. The captain seized his revolvers and threatened to shoot the first person who jumped into a boat. He set the men to pumping and bailing, and had provisions put into the boats which the women were to enter first by lot. All expected that the ship would soon go down. While the women sat with their wraps on, waiting to be called for the boats, little Arthur Douglas, unconscious of danger, was cheerfully singing, "There is a happy land, far, far away." "Do stop him!" said some. "No, no," said his mother, "let him sing." As the sea was calm, and the steamer had water-tight compartments, two of which were stove in by the collision, and St. Johns was but one hundred and fifty miles distant, by incessant efforts they were saved. How character comes out at such a time! Timid Christian women were calm and trustful; to one of them a sailor came and said, "My good lady, will you pray for me?" At the same time a passenger was heard swearing at the iceberg and using most horribly profane oaths. Another, a young man to whom I was introduced, was so wrought upon by the disaster that it was the means of his conversion to Christ.

Soon the Sabbath came, a pleasant day. The captain read the English church service in the morning, and the following sermon was preached in the afternoon substantially as here given. Many were present and very attentive. Prayers were offered by Rev. Dr. A. D. Gillette of New York, and Rev. J. S. Easton of Ohio. Two Scotch psalms were sung, being lined off.

SOJOURNING AND ITS PERILS.

Preached on the Steamship City of Washington, on the Passage from New York to Liverpool, Lord's Day, June 26, 1859.

I Peter i. 17.—PASS THE TIME OF YOUR SOJOURNING HERE IN FEAR.

SOME of you have recently been in great peril; brought face to face with what seemed the end of your life voyage! But you were mercifully delivered. It may very well be supposed that it is not without some apprehension that you and we all commit ourselves once more to the contingencies of an ocean passage—to a brief sojourn here. Our condition and relations may well awaken thoughts and suggest lessons of the way our souls are sojourning on the sea between the eternities.

The Apostle is speaking of the importance of holy living. He urges this upon his brethren from the character of Him who had called them into His service, quoting the command to His ancient people: "Be ye holy, for I am holy. And if ye call on the Father, who without respect of persons judgeth according to every man's work, pass the time of your sojourning here in fear." Be careful that you mistake not your own character, that you fail not of that holiness which secures the fellowship of God, and admits to the bliss of heaven. Peter urges the same thing, also, from the purity of Him who had redeemed them by His precious blood. Such is the text in its connection. Such is its force as a Divine caution. It contains also truths and intimations that deserve attention.

I. It declares us to be *sojourners*. Our present abode is but temporary. We are here only for a little time, and then pass on. It is a vivid picture of our earthly life, so transient, so soon over. We stay for a brief period, like one who visits a place, mingles in its scenes and with its people, and then departs; like a traveler who stops for a few hours or days in a place, and then goes on his way, and is seen there no more; like ourselves who meet and mingle and part on the short passage of an ocean steamer. David, from his royal throne and after a long reign said: "We are strangers and sojourners as were all our fathers; our days on the earth are as a shadow, and there is none abiding." Such is the universal experience. The first man, sinning, became a sojourner.

He could not remain in Eden. He could not stay in the world. He filled up his years and went away. Methusaleh, whose life was the longest of mortals, was only a sojourner. At length it was written of him, "and he died." His was a great age—almost a thousand years—how long it seems! But it was comparatively short. Few were the objects that filled his history; few the changes he witnessed. A life of sixty years now, with their varied and stirring events, is really longer than his. Noah, though he survived the deluge—the man of two worlds—was a sojourner. Moses and Joshua, the great leader and captain of Israel, in turn surrendered their commands and took leave of the hosts they had led. The Tishbite prophet, wondrous as was his power, and though spared the pain of death, was but a sojourner. God's chariot took him up from earth. All the great names of the past, immortal in the books of sacred or secular history, but represent sojourners here. They passed their time, and were not. Our blessed Saviour was a sojourner, "a poor way-faring Man of grief." He died. And though the feet of His risen body pressed the earth again, it was only for a little, and He ascended up from Olivet. But that or other mount shall no more feel the pressure of those feet till at the last day He comes for judgment in the clouds of heaven. The Pilgrim Fathers, Brewster and Winthrop and Williams were sojourners only. Such was Washington. He could not stay to witness the rising career of the country he delivered. The great gospel preachers of the past, sounding the trumpet-peal of redemption in the ears of men, and waking the slumbering churches to prayer and effort,—how short their lives! Luther had to lay off his armor and stop fighting the pope and the devil. Bunyan had to leave the immense congregations that hung with rapture on his inspired lips, and like his own Pilgrim pass beyond the river. Whitefield's clarion voice, that brought conviction and joy to thousands of hearts, died away from field and church. The great Edwards ceased after a few years to persuade men by the terrors of the Lord. Where are the ministers and the beloved pastors that many of us heard in our childhood? They were but sojourners. They are seen no more in the pulpit. Their voices and sermons only linger in our memories. So will it soon be with those who are seen and heard to-day. Where are the grandparents you can so well recall? The father, the mother, the brother, the sister, the friend, so recently with you? Oh, they were but sojourners here! How brief the stay of them! That little child, the other day so lovely, so sweet, so blooming, where is it now? Those tiny feet scarcely touched this earth, ere their patter was heard by angels on the golden floor. All are sojourners, every one of us, younger or older, passing our allotted time. And so are all we meet by the way, men of business, votaries of pleasure; the noble and Christlike, the mean and the vile; how soon each and all shall be with the past, with the generations of the dead! Oh, how near we are to the silent throng! Our brief Atlantic voyage from one shore to another is a symbol of life which, in the language of Job, passes away like the swift ships.

But Christians are sojourners in a peculiar sense. They confess themselves pilgrims and strangers on the earth. Here they have no continuing city. They seek a better country. Their citzenship is in heaven. In the world, they are not of it; chosen out of it, yet passing through it, singing, "We're homeward bound!" Those not Christians are no less sojourners, but they live here as if the world were their home. As all the home they have, they cling to it, but cannot retain it. They love it, but must leave it forever. It is as if one on the rail-car should look out on a tree or flower and set all his heart's affection on it. But he cannot stop to possess and enjoy it. He must pass away from it and come back no more. Poor worldling! no abiding place here—no home in heaven! To stop here is all his hope, treasure and joy; and yet he cannot stay. Though in the world and of it, he must be torn from it. He cannot detach one of the cars of time, throw it off the track, and make it an abiding habitation. No, the whole train is sweeping on through the world to the final terminus!

II. With this declaration that we are sojourners, is the intimation of another, a future and permanent life. "The *time* of your sojourning *here*." Beneath these words another world is disclosed. A star rises out of the depths of eternity, and directs our attention there. The very idea of a sojourner implies a region beyond the place of sojourning. One stops a few days at the springs, at the mountains, at the seashore, or goes to a foreign land; but when he ceases sojourning there, he is somewhere else. He has gone home. He is existing in another spot. We are now on the ocean, but a continent beyond awaits us. So if but sojourners here, we shall soon be elsewhere, in another state of being. Those who have got through with earth are somewhere in the great Hereafter, saved or lost. As this is true of all the dead, so it must be soon of all the living. It is this great and solemn fact that gives such a significance and underlying depth to the words—"the time of our sojourning here." Just beyond is Eternity! and we know not when we shall come to its threshold, or what step of ours will take us within its tremendous portal. Then the time of our sojourning is over. Then is reached the reality of a changeless existence. The infinite God is there, whose commanding voice echoed along the course of our pilgrimage, " Be ye holy, for I am holy." In the immediate presence of His majestic holiness how will sin and guilt appear? Jesus is there, the brightness of the Father's glory, the world's appointed Judge. Heaven is there, full of shining angels, full of white-robed saints, full of joy and free from sin. There all the saved live and rejoice. There the pilgrims and strangers have gone. There the ransomed sojourners go. Here to-day—there to-morrow and forever!

Nor is this all. Within the veil of eternity, close on the borders of this time of sojourning, is the dark and awful region of the lost. A day's march, an hour's journey, ay, a step, may reach it—an ocean wave, a sea-bubble—and then it is an endless experience and reality. That is the abode of those who made this world their pursuit and portion. There are the neglecters of God and their own souls, the rejecters of Christ and His salvation. There are those who chose delusions instead of divine truth, and who sought shelter in refuges of lies. There are the lovers of sinful pleasure, and hypocrites who wore the garb of religion, but lived in unrighteousness. There are those who put their hands to the plow, but turned back—those who were awakened, but delayed and died without repentance. There are the vile, drunkards drinking the wine of wrath, the lost and doomed, fallen spirits and Satan at their head. There they are in that world of woe, where the worm dieth not and the fire is not quenched. Oh, what unspeakable destinies, what amazingly glorious and awful realities crowd up and await us at the very verge of the limit of our sojourning here!

III. The relation of the present to that future life, and as a preparation for it, inspired the Divine caution in the text. "Pass the time of your sojourning here *in fear*." Be solicitous and anxious, for your character and work are subject to a holy scrutiny and judgment. In fear, not slavish, abject, tormenting; but filial, loving, obedient; that fear of God which is the beginning of wisdom, the essence of true religion, the beauty and glory of a life consecrated to Christ; which keeps faith a mighty power in the soul, hope its heavenly star, love its ruling element, obedience its practical result. In fear, of offending God who gave His Son for you; of wounding the Saviour who died for you; of committing sin, the soul's sorrow and ruin; of departing from the right way, of losing the joy of salvation, of failing of the rest that remains for the people of God. Hence, with a holy Being over you, heaven or hell before you, a tempting and ensnaring world around you, and besetting sins within you,—oh, fellow-voyagers, disciples of Jesus, "Pass the time of your sojourning here in fear." Several things urge this injunction.

1. Your liability to forget the reality and nearness of the solemn future, and your intimate relations to it. The world is ever around you, presenting its objects, and claiming your attention and regard. The things that are seen and temporal thicken about us like a cloud, and hide from our view the skies of eternity. Duty and necessity require us to mingle much in the affairs of the world, but we must guard against their gaining the mastery over us. We must not forget our higher errand and vocation. Our souls are in our charge. If Christians, we have assumed divine vows. We have taken the badge of discipleship, and have a commission from the Son of God. We must give account of our stewardship.

What if we should fail to meet our responsibility? What if we should stop to play with toys and sport with trifles, and overlook the grand mission and significance of our life and calling?

2. We should sojourn here in fear lest by a defective piety, or unworthy example, we hinder or misdirect others. None of us are so uninfluential, but some will be swayed by us, and will pattern after us; and they will not so readily perhaps copy excellencies as defects. Unless you habitually live and walk in the fear of God, some delinquency of yours may be a stumbling-block in another's path. It may darken the light of life in his soul, quench his zeal, hinder his usefulness, and cause him to err from the truth. It may confirm the skeptic, and keep the sinner from coming to Christ. How should one dread being the occasion of such injury and evil. Better that he sink with a millstone about his neck in the depths of the sea.

3. We should live in holy fear, lest we fail of the grace of God—lest, a promise being left us of entering into His rest, any of us should seem to come short of it. Not only the openly wicked will be lost, and those who never cherish any interest in the gospel, but some others will perish; some who have been awakened, some who have even professed religion; because they do not cleave

to the Lord and His people, because like the foolish virgins they have no oil in their lamps. Grace does not reign in their hearts. They love the world more than Christ. They are like the man in the parable who said, "I go sir," but went not. Paul had to strive and conquer, lest he should be a castaway. The Laodiceans, becoming lukewarm, were spurned as offensive to Christ. Judas, who had a position among the twelve, went to his own place as a son of perdition. Have not those ceasing to watch and pray fallen into temptation? Look at the rocks and quicksands where they have made shipwreck concerning the faith; where they have been lured to sin and folly; where they have sacrificed their religion and their souls. That young man—how full of promise was the opening of his Christian career! Where is he now! That young woman—how sacred were her vows; how beautiful her public recognition of them! How could she deny her Lord? Let him that thinketh he standeth, take heed lest he fall. Avoid the appearance of evil. Touch not the unclean thing. Neither give place to the devil. Keep yourselves unspotted from the world. Pass the time of your sojourning here in fear. Fear not them that kill the body; but fear Him which, after He hath killed, hath power to cast into hell; yea, I say unto you fear Him. Work out your own salvation with fear and trembling, lest God's saving pleasure be not wrought in you.

But is not the believer safe? Has he not assurance of salvation? Yes, he is, he has. But presumption or profession is not safety, and to be carnally minded is death. A Christian may wander and sin grievously. "And though," as Leighton says, "a believer is freed from hell, so that his soul cannot come there; yet some sins may bring as it were a hell into his soul for a time, and this is reason enough for the Christian in his right wits to be afraid of sin. No man would willingly hazard himself upon a fall that may break his leg or some other bone; though he could be made sure that he should not break his neck, or that his life were not at all in danger, and that he should be perfectly cured; yet the pain and trouble of such a hurt would terrify him, and make him wary and fearful when he walks in danger."

4. We should heed the caution of the text, for we know not when and where the time of our sojourning will end. You may be suddenly cut off. How near the end has seemed to some of you! If away from God, in the neglect of duty, in scenes of folly—there you may be called to die, and from thence, unwilling as you might be to have it so, your spirit be summoned to meet its

God. O brother! fear to depart from Christ and His service, lest, during such departure, death shall overtake you. Go nowhere, do nothing, in the midst of which you would not be ready and willing, if Providence so ordered, to die and render up your account!

5. Finally, the very greatness and grandeur of Christian responsibility—the soul's salvation in charge, eternal life embracing the fullness and duration of heaven—is sublime and glorious enough to inspire us with the profoundest solicitude and anxiety. What are we taking with us through this time of sojourning? What are we expecting at its close? Can we be thoughtless, careless, neglectful? Suppose a man is entrusted with a casket of jewels worth millions, and he must pass through dangerous places and among enemies and robbers on his way to the station where he is to deliver it in safety. Would he not guard his way and treasure with the utmost anxiety and vigilance? Consider the intense solicitude of the master of this steamship. Five hundred human lives are committed to his care. Vastly more than that number on two continents, with beating hearts and eager eyes, are watching this vessel charged with this precious freight. Great treasures in gold have been intrusted to him for safe transportation across the ocean.

What if he should be careless, faithless, reckless? How is his whole nature absorbed with the interests in charge! But are the work and responsibility of the Christian life, of an immortal soul, to which is committed this brief probation laden with all the amazing interests of eternity, any less momentous or important? If that soul fails, what a failure! If it succeeds, what a success! Is the gain or loss of a world any estimate of it? Can human language express it?

THE BEACON LIGHT.

WHILE on life's stormy sea
    My bark is driven,
From a fair coast to me
    Sweet light is given,
Gleaming around my way,
Cheering the dull delay,
Blending its golden ray
    With hues of heaven.

Clouds may o'erhang my path,
    Veiling the sky,
Tempests break forth in wrath,
    Billows roll high;
Still shines the one dear light,
Outlives the darkest night,
Brings morning calm and bright,
    Is always nigh.

That beacon light I have,
    And lose all fear;
The Saviour walks the wave—
    His voice I hear—

My precious, perfect Guide,
Bidding the storm subside,
Showing, beyond the tide,
   Skies heavenly clear.

I feel thy magnet powers,
   Bright world to come!
Faith sees thy glorious bowers,
   Where angels roam;
Where loved ones, gone before,
Now beckon from the shore
And make me long the more
   For them and home.

ENTRANCE TO THE HARBOR OF ST. JOHNS.
From "The Atlantic Islands," by permission of Harper & Brothers.

SERMON II.

PILATE'S QUESTION—OURS.

Dublin, Ireland.

PREFATORY NOTES.

THE two Sabbaths next following the one when the preceding sermon was preached, were passed in Ireland. On the first we attended services at Killarney, in the morning at the English church, and in the afternoon at a small Wesleyan chapel, whose minister urged us to occupy his pulpit. Dr. Gillette preached, and by request I gave some account of the great revivals the previous year in the United States. The congregation were deeply interested.

On reaching Dublin, we found the Irish Presbyterian General Assembly in session. We attended some of its meetings, and were treated with great kindness and hospitality. Rev. Dr. Kirkpatrick, in whose church it met, and whose assistant pastor was Rev. John Hall, now of New York, invited us to dine at his house. We were also furnished with tickets to breakfasts, provided by ladies at the Rotunda Hall for the whole Assembly. What added special and remarkable interest to the meetings, were the reports presented of the wonderful revival prevailing at the time all through the north of Ireland. Pastors and others had witnessed in three or four weeks more conversions than in all their lives before. Religious services day and night, in the churches and in the open air, were thronged with people, and scenes of the deepest interest, and sometimes of great excitement, occurred. We saw some of these field meetings in passing through the country.

The pastor of the principal Baptist church, Rev. Mr. Milligan, prevailed on us to stay and preach to his people on the Lord's Day. The sermon following was delivered on that occasion. At its close I gave some incidents of the precious revival in my church at home. After this service and that in the evening when Dr. Gillette preached, many lingered, and we sang several revival hymns and tunes that were new to them. The people gathered about us, and expressed very great interest in the privileges of the day, copied some of the hymns, and wished we could stay longer, and in revival meetings with them. The pastor from his pulpit, and in behalf of himself and his flock, expressed his great delight in the visit and services of his American brethren.

Rev. Dr. Cooke, the Nestor of the Irish Presbyterian pulpit, had desired to see us at his house in Belfast. As we called the Tuesday following, he insisted on our dining with him, after he had taken us over the city, to Queen's College, the Theological Seminary, in which he was a Professor, and to one of the immense linen establishments, and then wished we could stay longer that he might show us other things of interest. After dinner he walked with us a long distance to direct our way, and as we parted said, "God be with you."

PILATE'S QUESTION—OURS.

Preached in the Baptist Chapel, Dublin, Ireland, Sunday, July 10, 1859.

Matt. xxvii. 22.—WHAT SHALL I DO THEN WITH JESUS, WHICH IS CALLED CHRIST?

NOT for many years has there been in this land such an interest, such a profound solicitude as now, in this significant and suggestive inquiry. Christ seems to come how impressively near to the people at this hour, and His claims upon them are felt to be most serious and imperative. What mean the throngs by day and night, here in the largest buildings and there in the open fields, listening as for life to the gospel message? What mean the cries of hearts breaking for sin, and the rejoicings of new-born souls? We are reminded of the prophet's words: "Multitudes, multitudes in the valley of decision; for the day of the Lord is near in the valley of decision."

Pilate was in a position where he must take responsibility. He must act, he must decide one way or the other. He must do something with Jesus. He must protect and defend Him, or give Him up to his enemies. As the Roman governor of Judæa, Pilate was exclusively invested with the power of capital punishment ; and if Jesus is crucified, he must order or sanction the act. The Jews had condemned Him, and now the Gentiles through their judge, if he consents, will join them, that the whole world may crucify its Saviour.

From what he knew and saw of Jesus, His character and works, Pilate perceived that He was innocent, and to avoid responsibility said to the chief priests, "Take ye Him and judge Him according to your law." But this did not satisfy them; for they could not legally put Him to death; so they renew their accusations against Him. Pilate then put Jesus on trial, and at its conclusion said to the chief priests and the people, "I find no fault in this man." With a deepening conviction of His innocence, as the question came up, What shall I do with Him ? why did he not act the part of an honest and upright magistrate or judge? Christ's enemies still clamoring against Him, Pilate thought of another expedient. Incidentally learning that Jesus is a Galilæan, he sends Him to Herod who had jurisdiction there. Herod was now in Jerusalem, and glad of an opportunity to see Jesus, hoping to gratify a vain curiosity.

But Jesus wrought no miracle before him, nor answered any of his questions. Herod refused to take responsibility further than, with his associates, to mock and insult the Holy Sufferer and send Him back to Pilate.

The Roman governor is again troubled with the perplexing and momentous question, "What shall I do with Jesus, which is called Christ?" There was a conflict in his mind. He knew what he ought to do. He knew what justice required him to do. But there were false and furious men demanding that Jesus be given up to death. Shall he disregard their clamors and do his duty? Shall he be true and righteous toward the innocent Prisoner, or shall he deliver Him to his malicious foes? He seems hardly ready to do either. He calls together the chief priests, the rulers and the people, and tells them that as he finds nothing worthy of death in Jesus, he will chastise Him and release Him. He hoped this would satisfy the people. But they, following their leaders, called for the release of Barabbas. So Pilate could not escape his responsibility. He could not get out of his perplexity. The great question with him still was, *What shall I do with Jesus?* Something he must do with Him. And now was his time to do right, regardless of consequences. Why did he not say, "I know Jesus is innocent.

He has done nothing worthy of death: I will shield Him from the power of His enemies." Thus he should have done. But he had not the moral courage. So he takes a kind of middle course, scourging the innocent Jesus, with the hope that it might satisfy His foes. But after inflicting this act of cruelty, he grows morally weaker. He soon gives up Jesus, though not without some misgivings. "I find no fault in Him," he said, and repeated it, adding the words, "Take ye Him and crucify Him."

Thus Pilate, in the face of the clearest convictions of the innocence of Jesus, with a knowledge of his duty, the warning of his wife's dream, and the witness of his conscience, cowardly yielded his trust. He knew he was doing wrong. He was troubled and afraid when he heard that Jesus had made Himself the Son of God. He was somewhat horror-struck at the thought of his act, and that Jesus was something more even than an innocent man. It was not too late for him now to use his authority for the release of Christ. He goes to Him again. He confesses this authority: "I have power to crucify thee, and I have power to release thee." Why did he not exercise that power as his conscience bade him? He had this one more opportunity, and it was his last. "What shall I do with Jesus? I ought to release

Him." At this point, "the Jews cried out, saying, If thou let this man go, thou art not Cæsar's friend: whosoever maketh himself a king speaketh against Cæsar." On hearing this, Pilate brought Jesus forth and delivered Him to His foes to be crucified. Here was a matter of self, of worldly interest, rather than peril which, he is willing to doom the innocent Jesus to the death of the cross. Of what avail was it to wash his hands before the multitude, and utter the palpable falsehood: "I am innocent of the blood of this just person!" He was not innocent. He inquired "What shall I do with Jesus?" He confessed that he had power to crucify or release Him. And yet he gave Him up to be crucified. *That* is what Pilate did with Him who is called Christ. He did this though he knew that Jesus was just and pure, and he had intimations at least that He was the Son of God.

Perhaps I have dwelt too long on this action of Pilate. But the account of his course is instructive. Pilate is a representative man—a type of many others. The question of the text, as I observed at the beginning, is significant and suggestive. It was a serious, solemn and important question for the Roman governor to consider and to answer. It is a question of no less solemnity and concern to every one of us.

He could not avoid meeting it; nor can we. Consider then briefly, three topics involved in this question: WHAT SHALL I DO WITH JESUS? Under the gospel Jesus is *intrusted* to us all. We must do *something* with Him. What we do with Him *now* is an indication of what He will do with us *hereafter*. Such are our intimate and all-important relations to Jesus who is called Christ.

I. JESUS IS INTRUSTED TO US ALL. He is in a sense given us in charge. Pilate at that time was governor and judge; and Jesus came before him; was brought to him; he had Him on his hands, so to speak. In the gospel Jesus has come to us; He is brought before us; He is left on our hands. We are judges. We take the case; we must take it; there is no avoiding it. The responsibility is inevitable. The reality of it is as evident as our life, as our souls. Every one of us takes the charge of *life*—of living here in this world. We must take it. It is on us; and we must acknowledge and meet the charge. Every one has this life on him with all its mighty reality and meaning; with all its clustering interests and unutterable possibilities—its sublime joys and profound sorrows; its soaring hopes and shadowy fears; its privileges and its perils; its successes and its failures. And in regard to the soul, the great central and imperishable reality and significance of life, how may each say, "A charge to keep I have"! A man may think little of his soul, but he has it in his keeping. It is intrusted to him. He has got the precious jewel, the unspeakable treasure, and ever carries it with him. He cannot leave it. He cannot divest himself of responsibility in regard to it.

So it is with our relation to Jesus. We have Him in view. We have Him in charge. He has come to us. He has entered our very nature. Our flesh and blood He took. Oh, how intimate our relation! We have Jesus in the mysterious incarnation cast upon and incorporated, as it were, into our humanity, to restore it, to sanctify it, and to elevate it to the glorious and sublime realization of God's purposes and promises concerning His children. Thus we have Christ. Our race has Him—God incarnate! What a charge to be intrusted with!

Jesus was brought to Pilate, for his disposal. Jesus is brought to us, how often! Enemies brought Him to the Roman governor; but friends bring Him to us. The first desired His shame and death; the latter His glory and honor. Christian parents have brought Jesus to us in their instructions and prayers and example. Sunday-school teachers bring Jesus to those under their charge. How frequently they bring Him! And how often do Christians and converts, especially in this time of God's gracious visitation, bring Him to their friends? Not as those who took Jesus with staves and swords and thongs, and bound Him and brought Him to Pilate that he might scourge and crucify Him. No: they bring Him with tenderness and affection, with tears of solicitude and joy, that you may know, reverence and love Him. And what a trust every one, every child even, has in possession, to whom Jesus is intelligently brought!

Jesus comes to men in the Word of God. The *Bible* is full of Him. There you see Him, beautiful in the first promise, glorious in prophetic vision and utterance; at His birth heralded by the songs of angels and heavenly hosts, in His life and deeds gracious and merciful, in His death and resurrection speaking in righteousness, mighty to save. You that have the Bible are intrusted with Jesus. The blessed *Gospel* brings Him to you. We preach Christ and Him crucified. The ambassador of one nation goes to another and bears the will and purpose of his government and entrusts them to the authority there. So the ministers of Jesus bring His will and purpose, His messages and overtures to those they address. Nay, they bring Him to them. They bring Christ again and again, and entrust Him to their keeping. Jesus comes to men in every gospel sermon they hear. The *Holy Spirit* reveals Him—reproves, convinces, enlightens in regard to Him; so that men may know Him as the Saviour of sinners, as Pilate knew Him to be innocent. Conscience is quickened. Thought is busy. And men have to make up their minds as to the action they will take. Lost and sinful men have a Saviour given them. God so loved the world that He gave His only begotten Son. Jesus loved us and gave Himself for us. Oh, what a gift to all, old and young, rich and poor. Jesus is God's unspeakable Gift to you. He has intrusted Him to you. Pilate had Him before him, and you have the same Jesus before you. What will you do with Him? How will you discharge the sacred trust?

II. WE MUST DO SOMETHING WITH JESUS. All of us must. We cannot be indifferent. There is no neutral place for us,—no escaping the responsibility of action. Pilate had to dispose of Christ in some way, and so must we. He tried to get along without deciding, but could not. Nor can we. We are judges now. Every one is a Roman governor. Jesus is brought before you. He is on your hands, and you must dispose of

Him—must do something with Him. If you send him to Herod, he will send him back to you. The more you try to avoid a decision, the more you will find that such a decision must be made. If you postpone it for further conferences with Jesus, as Pilate did, the responsibility is not avoided. It comes back upon you with all its tremendous weight and solemnity. As the Jewish rulers and the clamoring multitude were awaiting Pilate's decision, and History was waiting to record it for all time; so your own interests, and men, angels and devils are awaiting your decision, and all your eternity will be shaped and colored by it. All men who know of Christ have this responsibility. When He was on earth it was so, from the time that Herod sought to kill the Holy Child, till at last He was slain by wicked hands. As He went about doing good, men everywhere either received or rejected Him, loved or hated Him, followed or forsook Him, called Him a Saviour or a sinner, Christ or Beelzebub. They did something with Jesus. The Nazarenes tried to throw Him down a precipice. Others sought to kill Him. Many heard Him gladly; hailed Him as the blessed and long-looked-for Messiah; were healed and saved by Him! Oh, how they worshiped and loved Him! What a welcome Guest at a house in Bethany! He had twelve chosen as Apostles. They had Jesus in charge. What did they do with Him? One betrayed Him—delivered Him up for a few pieces of silver. Think how Judas Iscariot disposed of Jesus, and what eternal infamy has blasted the name and the soul of that traitor! The eleven clung to Him. Peter for an hour or two denied Him, but bitterly repented, and served Him the more earnestly afterward. They proclaimed Him as the Saviour of men. They everywhere stood up for Jesus. They periled their lives for Him. They became martyrs for Him, as did thousands of others after them. When persecution raged, when Christians must renounce Jesus or die; then they had to choose what they would do with Him. When Saul of Tarsus saw the light and Form, and heard the voice from heaven, while going to Damascus; then he had to do something with *Him* who answered his inquiry: "I am Jesus whom thou persecutest." Agrippa, and Felix, and Festus, and thousands of others to whom the Apostles preached, had to do something with Jesus, as did the young ruler who came to Him with the question about eternal life; as did blind Bartimeus when Jesus of Nazareth passed by; as did the two thieves on the cross.

"What shall I do with Jesus?" You have already done something with Him. You have taken sides in regard to Him. I have; you have; all these Christians, veteran saints and young converts, have; and those still unconverted have. Those on the one side have received, and those on the other side have thus far rejected the Lord Jesus Christ. If I should ask one of these older Christians, a father or mother in Israel, what have you done with Jesus? the answer would be something like this: "Why, through infinite mercy and sovereign grace, years ago I was led to take Jesus to my heart. I took Him as my Prophet, Priest and King. He was made unto me wisdom and righteousness and sanctification and redemption. I put Him on by an open profession; I have observed His ordinances; I have tried to make Him my example and to do His will. I have put Jesus on the throne in heaven and in my heart. I love to sit at His feet and crown Him Lord of all. Unspeakably precious has He been to me, my Refuge, my Hope, my All." If I should ask these younger disciples and these happy converts, what have you done with Jesus? they would testify to a similar though shorter experience. They have endeavored to hear and do the sayings of Christ. They purpose now and ever to follow their blessed Lord. Dear souls, perhaps under temptation or in troublous times some of you have been or will be asking Pilate's question. Ah! what have you done, what will you do, with Jesus? Do not deny Him. Do not betray Him. Do not forsake Him. Do not wound Him in the house of His friends. Do not crucify Him afresh. Do not drive anew the nails into those hands that have been stretched out to save and welcome you, and into those feet that have run to rescue you from perdition. Do not pierce again that great heart that gave you its blood and beats for you with infinite love. Do not put another mock and torturing crown on that holy head that bowed in the agony of death for you. Oh! is it not enough that the thoughtless and wicked rejectors of Christ, the impenitent and unbelieving, should do this? Do not make any such compromises as Pilate sought, scourging Jesus by your worldliness, your errors, your indifference, confessing that you find no fault in Him, and then giving Him up! Oh, cling to Jesus now and forever! Sit at His feet, follow Him, obey Him, honor Him, all ye who have ever tasted His redeeming love and mercy. Let no name be so sweet, no love so strong, no service so absorbing, as *His*. Jesus, my Saviour!

> "Thy grace shall dwell upon my heart,
> And shed its fragrance there:—
> The noblest balm of all its wounds,
> The cordial of its care.

> "I'll speak the honors of thy name
> With my last laboring breath;
> Then, speechless, clasp thee in my arms,
> The Conqueror of death."

III. WHAT WE DO WITH JESUS NOW IS AN INDICATION OF WHAT HE WILL DO WITH US HEREAFTER. When the vacillating, dishonest and wicked governor gave up the innocent Christ to be crucified, that was not the last act of the drama. He was not through with the matter then, if he thought he was. That decision and disposal of Jesus had a bearing on another trial in another judgment-hall. Oh what a reversal! Pilate gives up Jesus, who soon dies on the cross. But not many years elapse ere the career of the Roman governor ends. Were they not years of remorse and sorrow! Did not the calm, sad, innocent, divine face of Jesus haunt him! Did not the flagrant injustice of his decision torment him day and night with reflections and forebodings more startling than the images of his wife's troubled dream?

Rising up in dark and frowning grandeur from the shore of lake Lucerne in Switzerland, is a high and gloomy mountain, over and around which almost continually hang lowering clouds and gathering storms. That is Mount Pilate, named after the wicked governor of Judæa who, according to tradition, having been banished to Gaul by Tiberius, wandered about among the mountains, stricken and goaded by conscience, until he ended his miserable existence by throwing himself into a lake near the top of this mountain. The unusual prevalence of clouds and tempests on it were long attributed to the unquiet spirit still hovering round the sunken body. When this was disturbed by any intruder, especially by casting stones into the lake, it revenged itself by sending storms and darkness and hail on the surrounding district. Be this all superstition, there is yet a foundation of truth in it—the common sentiment, that marked retribution follows a great crime; that punishment is sure to overtake the guilty.

At length, somewhere, the Roman governor died, and on his vision burst eternal realities. Then was not his guilt more clearly flashed upon him? He at once anticipates another day, another scene, another Judge. Time passes—time ends—and that awful day has come. Jesus descends to judge the world. Oh, what majesty and power, as He sits on the Great White Throne! See the Man of sorrows now—once the Prisoner before Pilate—see Him as the heavens and the earth flee away, and the graves are opened, as the dead rise, summoned to His bar!

But who is that coming to judgment, haggard, woe-begone, ghastly as the gates of hell? Ah! it is the Roman governor. Pilate is the prisoner now. He who once disposed of Jesus is to be disposed of by Him now. Oh, what a scene! what an interview! what a result! I can not dwell upon it. You can picture it to your own imagination.

But Pilate, as I said, is a representative man. We shall be there. We shall be judged by the Lord Jesus. We shall be disposed of by Him. We shall hear His kingly voice, "Come, ye blessed!" or "Depart, ye cursed!" according to our relation to Jesus here—according to our disposition or treatment of Him as He has come before us in the gospel. So our present choices and decisions will affect us hereafter—will determine our position at the judgment and our destiny forever. Those who serve Him here, He will honor there. Those who confess Him here, He will confess before His Father and the angels. Those who are not ashamed of Him here, of them He will not be ashamed when He comes in His glory.

Dear friends, how truly is Pilate's question ours! And it must soon be decided. He could not long parley or wait; nor can we. Now is a most favorable time to settle this momentous inquiry. The issue is rendered distinct by the wonderful revival of God's work in the land and here. Many have joyfully accepted Christ as their Saviour. Others, now that He is passing by, are seeking Him with the earnestness of the blind beggar at the wayside; with the earnestness of the woman of Canaan whose faith would take no denial. Seize the present opportunity. Decide the great question as you will wish it were decided when the prerogative shall have passed from you to Him before whose judgment-seat you must appear!

WHAT SHALL I DO WITH JESUS?

What shall I do with Jesus,
    The Christ, who may be mine?
Accept him as my Saviour?
    Or spurn the gift divine?
His only Son God gave me—
    I must, I do decide;
And Christ I take to save me,
    Or Christ is now denied.

What shall I do with Jesus,
    The precious Lamb of God?
I cast my soul upon him—
    He bathes it in his blood:
I'll gratefully confess him
    Before the vile and just;
My ransomed powers shall bless him,
    My sure and only trust.

What shall I do with Jesus?
    For him the cross I'll take;
All earthly losses suffer,
    Ere I the Lord forsake.

In scenes of joy and sighing,
    His love shall be the same;
While living and in dying,
    I'll glory in his name.

What thus I do with Jesus,
    When this brief life is past,
He will with me remember
    Before his bar at last.
Nor will he then disown me
    With those who hate and scoff;
At his right hand he'll crown me—
    He will not cast me off.

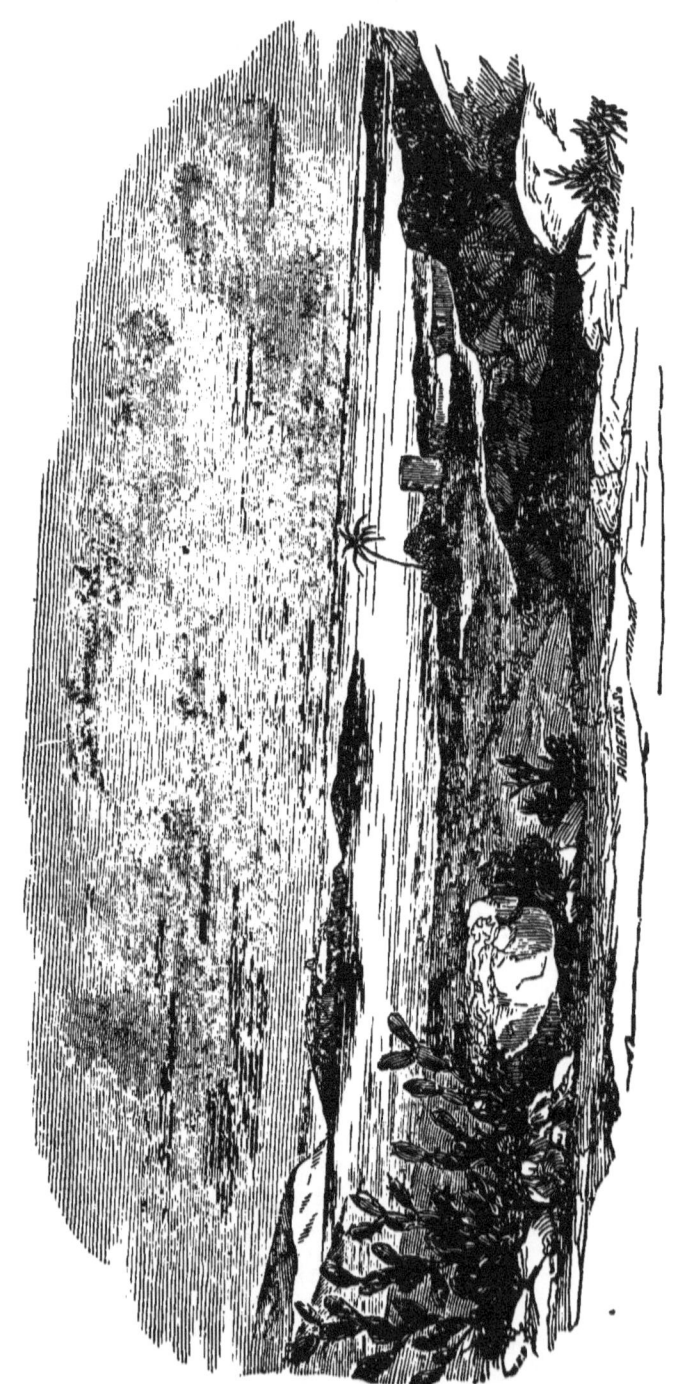

ST. PAUL'S BAY.

SERMON III.

OUR GREAT REFUGE.

Mediterranean Sea.

PREFATORY NOTES.

BETWEEN the preaching of the last sermon and the one following, six eventful months had passed. Very pleasant Rest Days had been enjoyed in many countries and cities, and among Christians of different names. The services varied from the simplest Protestant forms to the gorgeous and imposing ceremonies of a Christmas Sunday at St. Peter's in Rome. Nearly every Sabbath I had the privilege of attending at some place of Divine worship, and always found in it more or less of profit, even when an unfamiliar language was used. Some of those occasions and sermons are and ever will be remembered with pleasure. Among the preachers I heard were Dr. Candlish in Edinburgh, H. Stowell Brown in Liverpool, C. H. Spurgeon, W. Landels, and Dr. Cumming, in London, Dr. Heacock, (of Buffalo, N. Y.) in Paris, Dr. Malan in Geneva, and J. R. McDougal in Florence; and with most of them, including Dr. T. Raffles and Baptist W. Noel, I enjoyed most delightful interviews. The English church, in nearly every considerable place on the continent, has established a service and stationed a minister. Other denominations to some extent have done likewise. Travelers and others can thus worship in a way that is intelligent and familiar, and often with a church of their own faith and order. Tourists in large parties, embracing clergymen as they generally do, can extemporize a service on the Lord's Day, as was several times the case with us, and hence the preaching of most of these sermons abroad.

Embarking at Naples on a French steamer for Alexandria *via* Malta, we were soon on the Mediterranean sea and near places mentioned in Luke's graphic account, in the Acts of the Apostles, of Paul's memorable voyage from Cæsarea to Rome. As we approached the port of Valetta, where we landed upon the island of Malta, we passed not very far from St. Paul's Bay, the place of the shipwreck and marvelous deliverance of all who were on the stranded vessel with the prisoner-Apostle. Resuming our voyage, the island faded from view, and the open sea invited our passage to the wonderful and sacred lands of the old historic East.

As the Sabbath soon came, we had made arrangements for a religious service in the cabin, the captain of the steamship cheerfully giving permission. It was held at 11 o'clock, A. M. We began by singing, "Come, Holy Spirit," etc. Rev. William C. Child of Boston read from Acts xxvii. the very interesting account of Paul's perilous voyage upon this sea, and then offered prayer. We sang another hymn—" All hail the power of Jesus' name." Then was preached the sermon that follows these notes. At its close the two stanzas were sung, " From all that dwell below the skies," etc., and the service ended with a prayer and the benediction. Some of the three other ministers with us would have assisted in the worship by taking part, but for the rolling of the steamer and their tendency to sea-sickness. On the succeeding day we landed at Alexandria.

When in Beirût, Syria, I preached on Sunday, April 8, in the Mission Chapel at the request of Rev. Dr. Wm. M. Thomson, I repeated substantially this sermon.

OUR GREAT REFUGE.

Preached on a French Steamer, on the Passage from Naples to Alexandria, Lord's Day, January 15, 1860.

Romans viii. 31.—IF GOD BE FOR US, WHO CAN BE AGAINST US?

PAUL must have felt the force and comfort of the truth he here so tersely utters, when he sailed over this sea amidst great and terrible storms and dangers, and actually suffered shipwreck on the coast of that island our feet have so recently pressed. There was something sublime in his speech and prophecy, when he stood forth among his long-imperiled fellow-voyagers, and assured them of their safety on the presence and testimony of the angel of his God whom he served and believed. He was then on his way to Rome, where were gathered those disciples to whom he subsequently addressed the words of the text.

The whole chapter, of which they are so brief a portion, is singularly interesting and precious. It begins with the joyous declaration, that there is no condemnation to them who are in Christ Jesus, and it closes with the blessed assurance, that nothing shall be able to separate them from the love of God. These are delightful truths—glorious announcements. And how appropriate is the disclosure of such a Great Refuge to us, creatures of a day, waifs on the sea, surrounded by perils, lingering between two eternities, and soon to enter upon an everlasting destiny! GOD FOR US. Can we weigh the import of these words, or estimate the value of such an assurance? If God be against us, could we comprehend our position—the vastness of the difference between believers justified, and unbelievers condemned; between those who are in a state of salvation, and those who are in a lost condition?

The text has reference to the adopted children of the Lord Almighty, redeemed by the blood of Jesus, and heirs of eternal glory. Here they are servants of God, followers of the Lamb, pilgrims and strangers on the earth, seeking a city that hath foundations in heaven. They are subjects of the new birth; have repented of sin and believed in Christ; are loyal to their Lord, and living to do good; and so are building themselves up on their most holy faith, praying in the Holy Spirit, keeping themselves in the love of God, looking for the mercy of Christ unto life eternal. It is of such the Apostle asks, "If God be for us, who can be against us?" All true Christians may adopt this language. But what are its contents? How is God for us? I remark,—

I. GOD'S ATTRIBUTES ARE FOR US. His glorious attributes are all employed to secure the salvation of His people. His Wisdom was active in projecting the scheme of mercy. His Benevolence provided for the vast expenditure required for its execution. His Justice was manifest in the satisfaction rendered to the Divine Law by the suffering and death of Christ, that the believer might be justified. All the attributes of the Divine Being enter into the work of our redemption. But more particularly:

God's *Love* is for us. His infinite, His everlasting love is bestowed upon us—is the heritage of His children. The riches of this quality in Jehovah, who can estimate or fathom? We can form some idea of human affection. We know something of that sacred tie that unites us in the dearest and tenderest relations of life—parental, filial, wedded love—the affection that friend feels for friend, that one Christian heart cherishes toward another. We know something of what one will do for another, prompted by love—what the paent will do for a child; what interest he feels in its welfare; what sacrifices he will make for it. We know what a friend will do for a friend, at love's bidding—how that holy affection will endure through life; its pure flame, that many waters cannot quench, undiminished amidst all trials and changes. But this is only as the shadow of the love that God cherishes towards us—that love which began in eternity, is revealed in time, and endures for ever—the love that prompted Him to give His only and well-beloved Son; that gathers us into His own family and household; that saves us from sin and perdition; that unites us to Himself in the dearest relations; that purifies us and fits us for heaven and its joys; that makes us heirs of God, and joint heirs with Jesus Christ; that gives us the spirit and privilege of adoption; that brings us up from the dust to companionship with angels; that makes us younger brethren of the Redeemer; and that lavishes upon us the treasures of infinite grace. "Behold, what manner of love the Father hath bestowed upon us, that we should be called the sons of God." And that love is exhaustless and immortal. The human mind can not fully grasp it. Time can not compass it. Infinitude can scarcely measure it; for it is

"Eternal, fathomless, divine."

Yet it is for us—for all the children of God. Every trusting, filial soul takes shelter in it. Every anxious, wave-tossed heart can rest in it. Oh, what refuge is like Infinite Love!

God's *Mercy* is for us—mercy revealed in the Gospel, mercy for sinners, mercy which only God could show. It pitied our fallen state. It compassionated our guilty and hopeless condition. It looked tearfully upon our moral ruin. It sent the Saviour into our world of sin and death. It sang the song that was heard on the hillsides of Bethlehem. It spoke in the teachings and wrought in the miracles that the shores of the Sea of Galilee witnessed. It wept in the tears that fell at Bethany and Olivet. It groaned and bled and faltered not in the conflict and agony of Gethsemane. It struggled, endured and triumphed in the death of Calvary. It shines all-resplendent in the great Propitiation. It pleads all-powerful in the mediatorial Intercession. It pardons the penitent. It saves the believer. It welcomes every soul that comes to Christ. It is full and free, and all who will may receive it, even the chief of sinners. It is the Christian's inheritance; he shares it continually and forever. Its gracious arms enfold him, and draw him lovingly to the very bosom of God. This attribute is for us; and who can comprehend the mercy of God to men—His abounding mercy to them that love Him? "As the heaven is high above the earth, so great is His mercy toward them that fear Him." "As for man, his days are as grass; as a flower of the field, so he flourisheth; for the wind passeth over it, and it is gone; and the place thereof shall know it no more. But the mercy of the Lord is from everlasting to everlasting upon them that fear Him—that remember His commandments to do them."

God's *Power* is for us. Omnipotence is engaged in our behalf—pledged for our defence and safety. He is able to keep that which we have committed to Him. He is an Almighty Refuge. In His hands the weakest of His children are secure. He is their hiding-place and stronghold. Think of the power of God on our side! the power that piled up the everlasting mountains; that holds the billows of this boisterous sea and stills the tempest; the power that balances the universe upon nothing; that lighted up the sun; that scatters the stars and sustains them in infinite space; that erected the pillars of heaven, and garnished the mansions of glory; that peoples unnumbered worlds with intelligent beings, and ministers to their myriad wants. Think of that Power, joined with infinite Love and boundless Mercy, as pledged for us, and exerted in our behalf!

Love, as exercised by human beings, is often without resources to confer the blessings it prompts. Mercy may pity, but be unable to relieve. But the resources of Almighty Power attend these attributes of God. What would you not do for the friend you love, what blessing would you withhold, if the attribute of Omnipotence were yours? How, then, could you minister to the objects of compassion! Our God, who is for us, if we are for Him, has that unlimited power with infinite wisdom to direct its exercise. What a Friend we have to love us! What a protection He can give! How He can sustain in trial, and deliver from evil! What a shelter in our perils, and a defense from our enemies! Oh, to have the God of the universe for us, who can be against us? Who can harm us, or who can destroy us? How safe we are, how secure, how happy, let come what will, clouds, storms, shipwreck, we may feel as Paul did, buffeting the waves of this sea—There stands by us the angel of God, whose we are and whom we serve; and though the heavens fall and the earth be removed or consumed, we are safe in the hands of our heavenly Father. Oh, believer! "The eternal God is thy Refuge, and underneath are the everlasting Arms."

II. God's Providence is for us. How wonderfully He guided the prisoner Apostle over this storm-tossed sea, and delivered him and all those with him from the wreck on the island coast we lately left, and made every event of his voyage and trial advance his work for Christ and souls. God's superintending care is over us. The very hairs of our head are all numbered. Committing our ways to Him, He will direct our steps. He will lead us in the paths of righteousness for His name's sake. In this state of probation, of discipline and preparation for the life beyond, our heavenly Father may not exempt us from conflicts, trials and sorrows. He knows all the correction in righteousness, all the discipline of affliction we need. He knows how much prosperity we can bear, and how much adversity will be good for us. Health, sickness, privileges granted or denied—all these are ordered in infinite wisdom. And all things work together for good to them that love God. Circumstances that we may regard as a calamity, occurrences that may seem unpropitious, may be the very means that God takes to confer a blessing upon us. The darkest and coldest night brings out the brightest stars. Storms and tempests are necessary to purify the air. So piety often shines most sweetly in adversity, and afflictions refine the soul. Our Saviour was made perfect through sufferings. God knows how to bring good out of evil, and how to deliver the godly out of temptation. His all-pervading providence, His special superintendence is ever about us, is always for us, is never against us. We in our short-sightedness and lack of wisdom and faith, often murmur at Divine Providence as though it were a foe to us. Jacob mourns the loss of Joseph, regrets the absence of Simeon, and fears that Benjamin will be taken, and says, "All these things are against me," while God is using all those seemingly untoward events to bring about the most prosperous and joyous results. Thus all the dispensations of Providence, and those higher, profounder dispensations—the solemn decrees, the eternal purposes, the deep counsels of God, whether revealed or not—are all for us, and they are for all that put their trust in God. They furnish firm ground for hope, for confidence, and safety. Our Father has loved us with an everlasting love. And, in the words of an Apostle, "We are not appointed unto wrath, but to obtain salvation through our Lord Jesus Christ."

III. GOD'S WORD IS FOR US. The Bible pleads the cause of the Lord's people. It is on the side of the saints. It takes their part. It sustains and encourages them. Its glorious revelations are for them. Its prophecies and their fulfillments, its great and precious promises, the Saviour it describes, the salvation it unfolds, the heaven it reveals, the crown of glory it exhibits, are all for those that love and serve God. The commands and precepts of the Bible, and the rewards of obedience are ours. As we cling to the truths of Jehovah, which are as enduring as His throne, and unchangeable as His character, they will sustain and support us.

Human wisdom as a guide may lead us astray. Human opinions as a basis for religious belief and conduct may fail us at last—may be against us then. Not so the Word of God. Make it our guide, and no error deceives us; no delusion blinds us. Make the Bible the foundation of our life and character, and we rest on the Rock of Ages; we stand in the very strength of God—a sure footing, which nothing shall sweep away; which no assault can invalidate; which no convulsion can destroy. If we cling to the Bible, the Bible will cling to us, and defend us, and plead for us, and God will acknowledge the plea. The precious truths we have believed will uphold and comfort us, though all earthly aid should fail. The duties we have done and the practices we have followed, in the faith and love of Divine Truth—finding their appropriate outcome in practical benevolence and self-denying usefulness, will at last afford us unspeakable delight and joy. And what a serene, assuring satisfaction has the obedient believer! He has a spiritual insight and knowledge that reason and argument cannot give or overthrow. It is the witness of God in soul-experience. "If any man will do His will, he shall know of the doctrine, whether it be of God." Entrenched here we can sweep the voyage of life and eternity from a fortress stronger than the Gibralter that commands the entrance to this sea. The Bible as well as the God of the Bible is for us.

IV. GOD'S HOLY SPIRIT IS FOR US—the Spirit of all power, the Spirit of all grace. What a glorious Person to be employed in our behalf, to be enlisted in our defence. The Spirit that moved upon chaos at the creation, that evoked light from darkness, and order and beauty from emptiness and gloom; that inspired the song of the morning stars and the shouting of the sons of God; the Spirit that possesses every Divine perfection; that is the original Inspiration of Scripture, and the Source of wisdom and spiritual power; the world's Reprover of sin, of righteousness, and of judgment; the Author of regeneration, and the Sanctifier of the soul; the Comforter and Witness of the church; the Spirit that kindles, keeps alive and perfects the Christian graces; that abides in the heart and strengthens to trial and triumph the soul of every redeemed mortal; the Successor of the Saviour, and the Revealer of the things of Christ; the Enlightener of the mind, the Inspirer of prayer, and the Guide into all truth—that blessed Spirit is for us, if we walk in Him; and all His resources, His gracious and heavenly influences are pledged to sustain us, and promote our present and eternal good. With the gift, the graces, and the fruits of the Spirit, how can we fail, what can be against us, what can harm us, what shall separate us from the love of God? This is the Comforter that Jesus sends to abide with us for ever, and by Him we are sealed unto the day of redemption.

V. God's Son—the Lord our righteousness—is for us. The Saviour of the world, to whom is given all power in heaven and earth, is on the side of all His followers. He who wrought miracles in Judæa, healing the sick and raising the dead; He who resisted unto blood, vanquishing Satan, and rose in glorious triumph over death and the grave; He who came to seek and to save the lost, who was dead and is alive again and liveth forevermore to intercede for us, and is able to save to the uttermost all those that come unto God by Him; He is for us. And what has He declared? I am the Resurrection and the Life; he that believeth in me, though he were dead, yet shall he live; and whosoever liveth and believeth in me shall never die! Lo, I am with you always. He that heareth and doeth my sayings shall rest upon a rock that cannot be shaken. I give unto you eternal life. I go to prepare mansions of glory for you, and I will come again and receive you unto myself, that where I am there ye may be also. Ye shall eat of the tree of life in the midst of the Paradise of God. I will lead you unto living fountains of waters, and God shall wipe away all tears from your eyes. Oh, you shall be mine in that day when I make up my jewels; and my voice from the Judgment throne shall give you unutterable delight: Come, ye blessed of my Father, inherit the kingdom prepared for you from the foundation of the world. The Son of man who loved us and gave Himself for us, the Lamb of God whose blood cleanseth from all sin, the blessed Jesus in whom all fullness dwells, is for us, and He will never leave nor forsake us. Having loved His own, He loves them to the end. "My Lord and my God."

VI. God's Angels and Servants are for us. His people everywhere, all good influences, all good beings in the universe are for us. God's messengers of mercy and ministering spirits delight to watch over us, and in a thousand ways to aid us. The heirs of salvation are the favored subjects of angelic ministration and care. Far from home, in strange lands or tossed on the swelling sea, those unseen but holy and heavenly companions surround us by day and by night, God's blessed messengers of good to us. "The angel of the Lord encampeth round about them that fear Him, and delivereth them." The whole family of saints in heaven and earth are for us, are interested in our welfare, and linked to us by a holy and enduring affection. We are children of the same Father, redeemed by the same Saviour, renewed and sanctified by the same Spirit, and destined to the same eternal home. If nothing can separate us from God, nothing can separate us from each other. This blessed spiritual union will exist forever. All saints on earth are praying for us, and angels in heaven are rejoicing in our redemption.

In fine, all the resources of the Lord of hosts, who has the universe at His disposal, are for us. All that we know of Jehovah, all the treasures of His infinite love and benevolence, and all that we do not know of His boundless wealth and unsearchable riches of grace and glory, are pledged for the salvation and happiness of His people. Things that the unspiritual eye hath not seen, nor ear heard, nor heart conceived, are disclosed to us or reserved for our enjoyment. We may sometimes feel lonely and despondent, and think our foes are numerous and strong, but our faith may have the vision of a celestial army like that seen by Elisha's servant at Dothan, and the encouraging assurance comes, that more are they that are for us than they that are against us.

Hence, what a fullness of meaning is in the thought that God is for us. And if we are in heart and life on His side, "*Who can be against us?*" Not any good beings. Go where we will, if we are God's children, we shall be welcomed by those who love and serve Him; we shall share His protection; we are at home in His universe; we are in our Father's dominions. Jesus brings us into His banqueting-house, and His banner over us is love.

The Law is not against us, for it is fulfilled in the saints through Christ, who "is the end of the law for righteousness to every one that believeth."

God's Justice is not against us, for it is satisfied and its demands are answered in what Christ has done for us; and believing in Him we are justified by faith in His blood. "Their righteousness is of me, saith the Lord."

What if Satan, or the world, or death oppose us? Their opposition is unavailing. They are conquered foes. "Thanks be to God who giveth us the victory through our Lord Jesus Christ." Well might the Psalmist say, "When I cry unto thee, then shall mine enemies turn back: this I know, for God is for me."

While I can think of nothing more terrible, desolate, and appalling than to be unreconciled to God, to remain in disharmony with Him, to have Him thus against us—for a soul, by its persistent impenitence and rebellion and unbelief, to be abandoned of its Maker and only Saviour, to have no divine support in trial, no refuge in death, and no home in heaven—what solid ground the Christian has for entire confidence in God who is for him! Here the weakest may trust and rest and be strong. Oh, ye Fearings, Ready-to-Halts, Despondencies, and Much-Afraids, take courage! "He giveth power to the faint, and to them that have no might He increaseth strength. Even the youths shall faint and be weary, and the young men shall utterly fall; but they that wait upon the Lord shall renew their strength, they shall mount up with wings as eagles, they shall run and not be weary, they shall walk and not faint." How safe is he who has this Great Refuge. What peace, what happiness, what a destiny is his whose life is hid with Christ in God!

> " He feeds in pastures large and fair
> Of love and truth divine;
> Oh child of God, oh glory's heir!
> How rich a lot is thine!
>
> A hand almighty to defend,
> An ear for every call,
> An honored life, a peaceful end,
> And heaven to crown it all!"

Oh, friends, and fellow-voyagers on the sea of life, if any of you are fearful and full of doubt and uncertainty, destitute of heavenly love and trust, come into this Great Refuge, come to Christ the Ark of salvation, that shall outride every stormy wind and swelling wave, and rest at last on the bright immortal mount of God!

HYMN OF TRUST.

God is for me.—Ps. LVI. 9.

God is for me! oh, how glorious!
    Who the weakest saint can harm?
He will make that saint victorious,
    Held and sheltered by his arm.
      God is for me—
Nothing shall my soul alarm.

Wonderful the gift he gave me,
    Lost without a hope or claim;
Matchless mercy! when to save me
    Christ the Lord of glory came!
      God is for me,
Thanks eternal to his name!

Promises how great and precious
    Cheer and gladden all my way;
Peace and comfort, sweet and gracious,
    Keep me in their blessed sway.
      God is for me,
Guides and guards me day by day.

OUR GREAT REFUGE.

How his goodness round me brightens!
   His enfolding love I share;
Present help each burden lightens;
   Never fails his tender care.
     God is for me,
Nothing shall my trust impair.

All my heart this truth shall cherish,
   All my life, dear Lord, be thine;
Then, were earthly good to perish,
   Thy blest smile would on me shine.
     God is for me,
I am his, and he is mine.

When shall close this mortal being,
   When I reach the other side,
Oh, the joy, the bliss of seeing
   Jesus and the white-robed bride!
     God is for me,
Safe he'll bring me o'er the tide!

PYRAMIDS AND SPHINX.

SERMON IV.

THE TEARLESS LAND.

River Nile, Egypt.

PREFATORY NOTES.

MY first Sabbath in Egypt was passed in Cairo. I was engaged to preach for Rev. Mr. Barnet of the American Presbyterian Mission, but could not fulfill my engagement, owing to a severe illness which for three or four days kept me in bed. I enjoyed very much the society of this excellent missionary, and that of Rev. Mr. Lansing, also, who came on with our party from Alexandria. The next Sabbath, when the following sermon was preached, we were on the Nile. There were twelve of us, Americans, four being ladies. We occupied two boats, under the care of one dragoman, with whom we had contracted for a trip to Thebes and back. We had been but three days on the river, making only about a dozen miles a day, owing to head winds. We were in the company of those wonderful monuments, the Pyramids, looming up so grandly on our right.

This midwinter Sabbath was most beautiful. It was like the fairest of June days at home. We had arranged for a religious service at 11 o'clock, a. m., and the sermon was again assigned to me. We sang as the first hymn, "Majestic sweetness sits enthroned," etc. Psalm lxxxiv. and a part of Rev. vii. were read. Rev. W. C. Child offered prayer. After another hymn, "When I can read my title clear," etc., I preached on "The Tearless Land." Rev. Ransom B. Welch of Catskill, N. Y., followed with prayer. All seemed deeply interested, and several expressed their great pleasure in the service. In the afternoon we held a precious prayer meeting on the other boat. At its close, thinking of my dear flock in New Haven, I read over a list of their names.

How I came to preach this sermon, and be peculiarly affected by it myself, I hardly knew, unless it were that while I was ill at the hotel in Cairo, an American traveler died there of Syrian fever, having just come from Palestine, and whose wife and children were waiting for him in Geneva—a case that excited great sympathy. I might have had in mind also the sufferings of the Israelites from their oppressors in the very place where we were. In his prayer at the close of the sermon Mr. Welch, with deep fervor, besought sanctifying grace if any of us might have been bereaved.

How vividly all this Sabbath scene came in review when I learned five or six weeks afterwards, that *on the same Sabbath*, the funeral services of my youngest child, a bright, beautiful and darling boy of nearly four years, —in perfect health when I last heard from him—were held in my church at home, attended by a crowded and tearful throng. Ah! in God's providence there seemed to be an intimate relation between services and hearts so far apart and yet in a deep and tender sympathy so near together. Was it only a coincidence? Is there not sometimes a spiritual telegraphy vibrating with intimations, impressions, or intuitions from soul to soul, widely separated in space?

On the homeward Atlantic voyage on the American steamer Adriatic, being requested to preach Lord's Day, May 13th, I repeated this sermon, as there were among the passengers, a prominent citizen of New Haven, with the remains of his wife who had lately died in Paris; a young widow whose husband on the outward voyage had, while suffering from mental derangement, thrown himself into the sea, and others who had recently been bereaved.

THE TEARLESS LAND.

Preached in Egypt, on a Nile boat, in the vicinity of the Pyramids, Lord's Day, January 29, 1860.

Revelation xxi. 4.—AND GOD SHALL WIPE AWAY ALL TEARS FROM THEIR EYES.

HEAVEN is a frequent theme of the Bible. Gleams of its glory break upon us under various aspects and from different points of view. Clearer and brighter grow the visions of prophets and apostles, and more definite and animating their delineations of Heaven, as we trace the order and unfoldings of the Inspired Record. In its closing pages the pictures of the City of God are truly magnificent. We are there almost transported to the pearly gates; can almost see the jasper walls, and those within them; can almost hear the new song and the heavenly harps; and in that light surpassing the sun and the moon, we can almost behold the ever-blooming tree of life in the midst of Paradise, and the crystal waters of the river flowing out from the throne of God and the Lamb. Thus the Bible begins and ends with a Paradise, the one earthly and the other heavenly. But what a world lies between the two; what strange events, conflicts, and perils; what a history is there; what glooms hang over it; what lights relieve it! It is a history of Paradise lost, and Paradise regained—extending through this long and sad vale of tears. And how much more a vale of tears this world would be, were it not for the influences, thoughts and hopes of that world where all tears shall be wiped away.

Among the varying aspects of the blessedness of Heaven, as presented in the word of God, are its positive enjoyments; its actual attractions and glories; its inheritance incorruptible, undefiled, and that fadeth not away. Then it is set forth and rendered no less alluring to us, as the place where all evil will be absent; where every thing that injures, pains, disturbs and annoys us here, will be excluded; where the inhabitant shall not say, I am sick; where nothing that defiles shall enter; where sighing and sorrow shall flee away; and where there shall be no more death. Heaven has attractions for all Christ's followers—something just adapted to their desires and wants—no matter what their condition is here as to trials, sufferings and losses. It has riches for the poor, rest for the weary, home for the pilgrim, joy for the sorrowing, society for the lonely, eternal safety for the trembling.

No Tears in Heaven! How different from this world! What floods of tears have moistened the earth in every age! Who, of all its millions, has not at some time wept? What multitudes have wept bitter and burning tears of sorrow and grief? How many, while we may rejoice, are weeping now in anguish, and some it may be in the homes we have left far away! And how many will weep and weep on, long after our last tears are shed.

> "In heaven alone no sin is found,
> And there's no weeping there."

Not so on earth. Nor have any class been exempt from tears. The best, happiest, most favored, have not been utter strangers to weeping. *Jesus wept*—wept at the grave of Lazarus, wept over Jerusalem, wept in the Garden, wept over the effects of sin and over souls rushing to their doom. He, Man as well as God, wept in sympathy with the infirmities of our nature, for He could be touched with them. Alexander wept; but how different his tears from those of Jesus. All men weep at times. Nor do we envy one who never weeps. There is often a solace and a sympathy in tears that bring or give relief. But they always imply sin or sorrow, and hence indicate our fallen state. There were no tears in Paradise till transgression brought them. There will be none in Heaven, that state of sinless purity and perfect happiness. The saints in light will never mourn. "And God shall wipe away all tears from their eyes." But He does not promise to wipe away all tears here. Nay, we are to weep with them that weep, in imitation of our blessed Lord. "Weep for yourselves and your children," said Jesus on the way to Calvary. There are many kinds of tears shed here—many occasions to unseal their fountain—times when they cannot be restrained. But there will be no occasion for them in Heaven. Drops of grief can never fall on the golden streets, or in the celestial mansions. God will wipe away from His peoples' eyes every kind of tears.

He will wipe away the tears of *Penitence*. Penitential weeping! It appeals to our heavenly Father. It moves His pity and wins His forgiving love. Jesus looks with peculiar regard upon the penitent. The poor publican who bowed himself to the earth and doubtless with weeping cried, "God be merciful to me a sinner," received at once the Divine favor. The most blessed tears, those which Heaven regards with the deepest interest, are the tears of penitence—weeping over sin, over its guilt in the sight of God, over its ruin of the soul—weeping because Infinite Goodness has been disregarded, and infinite gifts of love and mercy despised; Jesus knocking at the door of the heart, but shut out till now. Oh, how are the fountains of the heart unsealed, its great deeps broken up, and the soul itself seems to dissolve in penitence, when at length the sinner bows and yields at the cross of Christ, truly a subject of godly sorrow, and repentance unto life. Whether tears always flow at such a time, there is surely a feeling kindred to them.

But all tears over self-guiltiness are not tears of true penitence. There is a beatitude of sorrow, and a sorrow of the world that worketh death. There is such a thing as seeking repentance with tears, and yet no full surrender of the heart to God—no decisive choice of Christ and His service. Many, convicted of sin, have wept, and struggled with their consciences, and yet have been unwilling to let go the world and follow Jesus. God does not promise to wipe away such tears in the future world; but tears of those who have truly loved and served Him here, lamenting their sins and imperfections, and often it may be shedding penitential tears for their departures from and momentary denials of Christ. How bitter were Peter's tears after his denial of his Lord! While Christians live in this world they will never cease to see sins and imperfections to weep over; and because they do weep over them, because they are penitent, cleaving to the Lord in faith and prayer and righteous toil, He will wipe away all such tears when they enter Heaven. No more will they grieve and repent; no more will they mourn their want of likeness to God; for the former things are passed away. Every trial is over; every conflict is ended. And what a blessed state that must be—what a glorious world—where there is no weeping! We wipe away our tears, but they come again; occasions are constantly occurring to cause them to flow; but when God shall wipe them away, they come no more!

All tears of *Sorrow* shall also be wiped away. I speak of sorrow now in a general sense. And how much of it there is and always has been in this world of sin! How much of it in this green valley, when these Pyramids were reared by exhausting human toil; when the Israelites performed their hard tasks here under the iron hand of the oppressor; and when their infant children were hunted and slain, and Moses was spared only by the compassion of a princess moved by his weeping as she found him in his ark among the flags of this river. Not a day passes now, not an hour, not a moment, but some heart is breaking, some soul is in anguish, some eyes are suffused with tears. Much of this sorrow is public. We meet it every where on this sin-blighted and woe-stricken earth. "Man goeth to his long home and the mourners go about the streets." Injustice, oppression, cruelty—these, as well as sickness and death, cause hearts to bleed. Idleness, dissipation, crime—these bring innumerable sorrows in their train; often the innocent are involved, and so suffer and weep. Even the circles of gayety and pleasure, of fashion and vanity, often leading to sin and guilt, are not free from sorrow. The forefront of the picture may seem all gladness and bliss; but there is a dark background of remorse and pain. "Sorrow lives with those whose pleasures add unto their sins." There are depths in the ocean never measured, never seen; so there are depths of grief and woe in the heart that the world neither sees nor knows. "The heart knoweth its own bitterness." Many tears are secretly shed, many pangs felt alone. Many troubles choose concealment.

> "Great sorrows have no leisure to complain;
> Least ills vent forth; great griefs within remain."

God's people are not exempt from trials here. There are times when they have sorrow upon sorrow. "In the world ye shall have tribulation," said Jesus. Prophets and Apostles have wept. Christians experience various kinds of sorrow—now and then passing through a valley of Bochim. But theirs is a chastened grief. Theirs are not tears of despair. No—there is a blessed sunrise after a somber night. There is a beautiful bow spanning the dark cloud. There is a sweet voice alternating with the thunder in every storm, and heard above the waves in every rough sea, "It is I, be not afraid." But, oh, blessed thought! all their sorrows and all their tears of sorrow shall be left this side the gate of Heaven. God's own soft hand will wipe them away. Their hearts shall no more be heavy, their eyes no more dim. Saints will see in each other's faces in Heaven the light of peace, the glow of joy, the sparkle of bliss; but they will never see there the lines of grief, the shades of sorrow, or the tears of sadness. There will be no secret chambers of mourning; no silent, concealed anguish; no weeping over private woes. How glorious is Heaven considered in its negative attractions—a place where all evil is absent; where sighing and sorrow and tears are never known; where, freed from sin, we are freed from every ill!

Again, there are no tears of *Disappointment* in Heaven. There are many of them in this world; but God will wipe them all away from the eyes of His children there. They can never know a disappointment. They are beyond such a possibility. They will continually be surprised and delighted by the opposite of disappointment. The queen of Sheba, coming to see the splendors of Solomon, said in astonishment that the half had not been told her. But what were that queen's emotions when, if admitted to Heaven, she beheld the glories of the celestial city! No, not the half, nor even the outlines of a blessed immortality can be perceived or comprehended by the holiest saint in this world. None of the promises of God with reference to Heaven will fail. None of the Bible descriptions of its beauty and bliss can possibly fall short of the reality. None of the Christian's hopes and anticipations of its glory exceed the truth. No—unthought-of, unspeakable, and uncomprehended joys, treasures and attractions will burst upon the vision of the believer as he enters Heaven. He cannot be disappointed there. But here in this world he may be. Grievous and bitter may be his tears at some sudden reverse, some heart-breaking loss, some unexpected grief. A friend, too confidently trusted, may deceive; may prove false; may involve us in trouble; may crush our earthly hopes. We know not what disappointments a day may bring forth; what tears we may shed to-morrow; what unlooked-for adversities may overtake us. The Christian is in great measure prepared for these, if they come, by his trust in God and His providence, though he may not escape the effects of disappointment, or prevent the tears it may bring. Oh, how much of suffering and weeping in our world may be traced to this source! Disappointment has broken many a heart, and filled all its after earthly life with sorrow. But there is none of it in Heaven. Its tears are all dropped this side of the Celestial Gate. All the disappointed will not enter Heaven; but all who do enter, will be disappointed nevermore.

God will wipe away, too, all tears of *Bereavement* from the eyes of His children. What, more than affliction, the inroads of death, the loss of relatives and dear friends, makes this world a vale of tears? Tears of bereavement—who has not shed them? What family circle has not at some time been a mourning group? Who of us has not followed some dear one to the grave? How often has the tear-drop fallen over the lifeless form, on the new tomb, or flowed in sympathy with others sorely tried? Very often are the familiar lines on our lips:

> "Friend after friend departs;
> Who hath not lost a friend?
> There is no union here of hearts,
> That finds not here an end."

Many a mother, like Rachel, has mourned for her children and refused to be comforted, because they are not. Many a father, like David, has said in anguish of soul, Would God I had died for thee, my son; and has felt, like Israel, that his grey hairs would go down in sorrow to the grave. Sisters, like those of Bethany, have mourned a brother's death; and widows like her of Nain, have seen their only child and earthly stay taken from them. Go where we will, dwell where we may, bereavement everywhere meets us. In all our journeyings we see indications of it. There is no day, no night, no hour, but some house is a house of mourning; from some eyes drop the tears of affliction. All the while there is somewhere a sad and sorrowing procession slowly marching to the grave. The unsightly hearse is always moving, unlading at the tomb its burden, and returning to bear thither another. Some all day and all night are watching at the bedside of the dying. Silence and death come, welcome or not, into homes and rooms where joy and gladness had been. The grave-digger's work is never finished.

What if all this should stop for a while! Death cease his work; no more digging of graves; no more bereavement; no more tears for the departed! What a wonderful change! How striking the effect! And yet earth would not then be like Heaven. Sin would be here. Tears would still fall. A curse and doom would hang over the world. Antediluvian longevity was not favorable to piety. But how are we impressed with the happiness and the glory of Heaven, when we think of the sublime declaration, *"There shall be no more death!"* No tears of bereavement there; no parting with those we meet there; no sickness; no couch of pain; no mortal agony; no corpse ever seen; no funeral procession; no grave ever dug. It is appointed unto man *once* to die. And when the Christian has gone through that solemn scene, he looks *back* upon death as past for ever! The reign of mortality is left, with all its ills, its perils, its pains, its sorrows, its tears. Oh, what a transit! How must the soul thrill with new and wonderful emotions! An angel's wings, an angel's strength, and more than an angel's joy, it has. I am now immortal. Death cannot reach me. *I am in Heaven*—the tearless land, for which I hoped and longed, and prayed to be prepared. What glories surround me! What sights and sounds! What beings I behold, what friends I meet! Never shall we part. Infinite happiness! Unutterable glory! Before me, around me, every where, it is Heaven, it is Heaven! Oh, there is Jesus, who loved me and gave Himself for me, and washed me from my sins in His own blood. Let me go and bow at His feet, cast there my crown, and adore Him. I see the land that was afar off, and the King in His beauty. Allelujah! Glory and honor and blessing and power to the Lamb for ever and ever!

Further, God will wipe away all tears of *Anxiety* from the eyes of His children. But such tears will always be shed in this world. Jesus Himself wept them over rebel sinners, over a doomed city. What deep solicitude do Christian parents feel for the welfare of their children. Some have not yet given their hearts to the Saviour. Perhaps they manifest aversion to religious things. They are captivated with the pleasures and vanities of the world. Their precious souls are in peril. Prayers are offered and tears are wept in secret places for them. Ministers feel thus, weep thus, over the impenitent and wayward in their congregations. The course of the wicked is always a grief to the people of God. "Rivers of waters run down mine eyes, because they keep not thy law." Jeremiah is called the weeping prophet because he mourned so over the waywardness of his people. "Oh that my head were waters," said he, "and mine eyes a fountain of tears, that I might weep day and night for the slain of the daughter of my people." When Elisha perceived the wickedness that was in Hazael's heart, and the results to which it would lead, "the man of God wept." Christians often weep with sad anxiety over those who persist in their neglect of the gospel and their souls. Shall they go heedless or headlong to ruin, awaking at last to a full realization of what they have done and lost, lamenting their course in the unavailing tones of a settled and ever-deepening despair: "The harvest is past, the summer is ended, and we are not saved"? Such anxiety moved the mighty heart and yearning pity of the Redeemer, and He wept—wept over the doom of the unbelieving rejecters of Him and His grace.

Disciples of Jesus feel often a profound solicitude in reference to the results of their labors in the vineyard of the Lord. They must give an account of their stewardship; must answer for talents given. They cannot shake off responsibility. How will they appear at last? Who has believed their report? The Sabbath school teacher is anxious for the conversion of the class so often met. There is many a weeping sower in the service of the great and blessed Taskmaster; and how cheering the promise, "He that goeth forth and *weepeth*, bearing precious seed, shall doubtless come again with rejoicing, bringing his sheaves with him." Many are painfully anxious about the welfare of Zion, and concerning their own spiritual state. Tears are shed in self-examination and because so little progress is made in grace and holiness. But in Heaven there are no such tears; no weeping sowers there; no anxious, trembling laborers; no painful solicitudes are felt; no rivers of Babylon to sit down by and weep. All this is past. The work-day of probation is gone by. Each toilsome task is done. An eternal day has dawned. All is reward now. The glad *welcome* at Heaven's gate into the joy of the Lord, is the final *farewell* to anxieties, toils, and tears. Oh blessed release! Oh infinite reward! This glorious prospect is enough to encourage and animate us in all our duties here. Think of what awaits us in Heaven!

"'Tis then the soul is freed from fears
And doubts which here annoy;

>   Then they that oft had sown in tears,
>   Shall reap again in joy."

There are, again, no tears of *joy* in Heaven—no *tears* of joy. On earth sometimes such tears are shed. Sometimes even for joy and gladness we lift up the voice and weep. Some sudden, unlooked-for delight—some narrow escape, some dreaded crisis past, some friend saved from peril or met after a long absence, some powerful emotion, or rapturous, sympathetic feeling—has brought the gushing tears from our eyes, and they mingle with our smiles, like the shower in the sunshine. But in such tears there is some admixture of sadness or pain; something is connected therewith that made us fear and tremble; something that showed an imperfection in our happiness. If there were no tears but those of joy in our world, it would be greatly changed; but it would not be Heaven—far from it. But when God takes His people there, He will wipe away *all* tears from their eyes. Even tears of joy within the immortal gates would mar the perfection and diminish the blessedness of Heaven; so they will be left behind.

Finally, God will wipe away all tears of *Painful Apprehension* from the eyes of His children.

Not one such tear shall be wept in Heaven. How thickly they fall in this world! What sorrow, uneasiness, dissatisfaction and foreboding they betoken! David had the emotion they indicate when he said, "I shall one day perish by the hand of Saul." The Christian, not having attained to perfect assurance, knows what the feeling is. He loves to think of Heaven. It is pleasant and delightful to meditate on its glories. But, when he thinks of the worldliness that clings to him; the sins that easily beset, and are so hard to conquer; so much in his heart unsanctified yet; his small measure of love to God; his dilatoriness in Christ's service; his slow progress in the divine life; his unworthiness of God's mercy and salvation; the poor returns he makes—all this causes him at times to apprehend a denial at Heaven's gate; a rejection when the Lord shall make up His jewels in the last day.

> "When thou my righteous Judge shalt come
>   To take thy ransomed people home,
>   Shall I among them stand?
>   Shall such a worthless worm as I,
>   Who sometimes am afraid to die,
>   Be found at thy right hand?"

No—he is almost ready to say—I fear I never shall stand there, clothed in my Saviour's righteousness, and hear His blessed welcome to a glorious and everlasting kingdom. And yet I cannot bear the thought of my name being left out of the Book of Life. I cannot bear the thought of being forever separated from Jesus and Heaven. Why art thou cast down, O my soul? Hope thou in God; for I shall yet praise Him. The imperfect believer has many apprehensions concerning death and the judgment. Shall I not be surprised and overwhelmed when I come to die? Shall I then be sustained by Jesus' presence and grace? Can I calmly, hopefully endure then? Can I triumph over the last enemy? Yes, dear disciple! Christ will give you dying grace which you do not need till that hour comes. He will be better than your fears. He will cause you to rise above your apprehensions. He will bring you to Heaven. "He that hath begun a good work in you will perform it until the day of Jesus Christ." Then, farewell fears, and all forebodings! Farewell all painful anticipations! There is nothing more to dread in the future; nothing gloomy there; nothing to be apprehended with fear and trembling. Oh what a relief, what a joy, to feel that we are safe forever; safe *in* Heaven; delivered from all sin, all sorrow, all tears. So, dear disciple of Jesus, you will feel, when you find yourself *within* the Celestial City.

I have but little time for the lessons of this subject. Behold the contrast between Heaven and Earth—between this tearful vale and that tearless land. Oh, Christian! can you cling to earth? Can you fail to be heavenly-minded? Can you be absorbed with the interests of this world, to the neglect of the infinitely superior interests involved in the glory to be revealed? Can you strive for things temporal and pleasures fleeting, and overlook treasures eternal and joys undying? Can you compare the dross of earth with an immortal crown? Think more of the tearless land. Let its precious and powerful attractions draw you thitherward.

Behold, also, the greater contrast between Heaven and Hell. If there be such a difference between the house of the saints' pilgrimage here, and their eternal home in glory; if earthly dwellings are so unlike the heavenly mansions; who can set forth the wide disparity, the infinite contrast between the future abode of the righteous and that of the wicked? No tears in the world of light. Not so in the world of outer darkness. There, "there shall be weeping and gnashing of teeth." No soft hand shall ever wipe those burning tears away. They will flow for ever. There the lost will weep for anguish; weep over wasted opportunities; over squandered time; over deferred interests; over wicked choices; over fatal neglects; over final separation from all that is good and blessed in the universe. Think of such weeping for a long eternity! No relief, no end, no God to wipe those tears away; no Saviour to redeem your soul! Oh friend, can you go to such a doom?

Learn, Christian, to adore that Grace that saves you from a lost condition, and exalts you to Heaven. Remember, it is God who wipes away the tears of His children. They could not do it; they could not quench them. No works, no sacrifices, no sufferings of theirs could ever dry up the fountain of their grief. It takes a God to do it; an almighty Saviour; an infinite Sacrifice— Jesus, the dying Redeemer. Through His recovering mercy, by faith in Him, we rise to the tearless world. Oh what love and gratitude we owe to Him!

Learn again, that, if all tears are to be wiped away in Heaven, we can afford to weep and labor and suffer here, and make sacrifices, if our Lord requires them of us. We can bear any trial, do any service, endure any hardness, submit to any cross, for His dear sake, however humbling or painful, seeing the time is so short, the sorrow or toil will soon be over; and then, then—*what?* An eternal weight of glory! Heaven, all Heaven, and no tears—no more grief! Let thoughts of that tearless home mitigate our sorrows or turn them into joys, inspire our faith, cheer and encourage our hearts, prompt us to duty and wean us from earth.

Learn, also, all of us, the importance of a preparation for Heaven. It is sin that makes tears; and sin must be got rid of. It is unreconciliation to God that makes us unfit for Heaven; and we must be reconciled to Him. We must be born again; we must be new creatures in Christ. Is Heaven begun in our hearts? It must be begun there, or we shall not be prepared to enter its gates and enjoy its glories hereafter!

NO TEARS IN HEAVEN.

And God shall wipe away all tears from their eyes.—Rev. vii. 17.

No tears in Heaven! Oh, blessed thought!
City of God with beauty fraught,
Who can its wondrous things unfold,
Its jasper walls and streets of gold,
Its harps and crowns and robes of white,
That thrill the soul and charm the sight,
Where shines a radiant endless day,
And every tear is wiped away!

How oft is wept by mourners here
The humble penitential tear!
Nor does the Lord disdain such grief,
But gives through faith a sweet relief.
Angels delight at tears thus shed
By souls that hence are heavenward led;
When hither called, and entering in,
They weep no more o'er self and sin.

THE TEARLESS LAND.

What floods of sorrow rise and flow,
Where hearts their bitter anguish know,
By deep bereavement sorely tried,
As every earthly fount seems dried.
But all these streams of trouble cease,
And souls find sweet unbroken peace,
As to their rest they soar on high,
Where tears are wiped from every eye.

Life seems a wasting scene of care,
To hearts that anxious burdens bear;
Tears fall o'er disappointments sad,
And scarce a day is bright and glad.
Oh, happy change! when e'er 'tis given
To pass the gate that opes to Heaven!
No boding thought e'er shades the mind
Where every tear is left behind.

Nor there those crystal drops that here
Sometimes as tears of joy appear,
For every weeping night is past,
And morning joys shall ever last.
Immortal land of life and light,
Home of the saved forever bright,
Blest world of love, sweet realm of bliss,
Free from the tears that fall in this!

JERUSALEM FROM THE NORTHEAST.

SERMON V.

CHRIST ALONE.

Mount Zion, Jerusalem.

PREFATORY NOTES.

AFTER a six weeks' trip on the Nile, a visit to the Red Sea and the Wells of Moses, a short voyage from Alexandria to Jaffa, the ancient Joppa, brought the Holy Land into view. The next day a long-cherished dream was fulfilled—my feet stood within the gates of Jerusalem! The third day after was the Lord's Day. This Rest Day is sweet to the Christian any where; a day of cherished privileges, holy memories, and blessed anticipations, a type also of the rest and worship of Heaven. But what hallowed associations cluster around a Lord's Day in Jerusalem! What thrilling and tender scenes from the past crowd upon one's thoughts as the very places where they occurred are beneath the eye!

I arose that clear, calm and beautiful morning and looked out at the east window of my temporary abode on Mount Zion; the sun was just rising gloriously over the summit of the Mount of Olives. I thought of the event of that brighter morning, inaugurating and crowning the Lord's Day, when, just at my left, the place in view, the Sun of righteousness arose from the darkness of that tomb at the foot of Calvary. Toward Olivet about midway stood the Mosque of Omar, occupying the very spot of the once splendid and sacred Temple, so often greeted by the same rising sun.

Several of our party had arranged for an early walk around a portion of the city outside its walls. Passing out of the Jaffa or Bethlehem Gate, on the west side of the city, and descending southward by the Lower Pool of Gihon we were soon in the deep Valley of Hinnom. We sat down on the farther slope to rest a little while under the shadow of a great rock. Above and back of us was Aceldama, and directly in front on the north was Mount Zion. Occasionally wheat-fields and olive-trees were on the broad slope, but no buildings were in sight. Once the city covered that hill with dwellings and palaces, but in the striking fulfillment of prophecy it has become a plowed field. We sang one of the songs of Zion, and went down the valley to its junction with that of Jehoshaphat, passing amid ancient tombs and rocky defiles the place of the horrid rites of Moloch. Drinking from the Well of En-Rogel, we turned northward and went up the Valley of Jehoshaphat, between the city and Olivet. We passed on our right the tomb of Zachariah and the Pillar of Absalom; on our left the Fountain of the Virgin and the Pool of Siloam. Through this valley flows the brook Kidron. Entering the city at St. Stephen's Gate, we passed up the *Via Dolorosa* going close by and just south of Calvary, and soon reached our hotel. Later in the forenoon we attended upon services at the English church and heard a sermon from Bishop Gobat.

In the afternoon, going through Zion Gate, we walked along by the city walls south and east, looking at some of the great stones at the corner, laid probably as early as Solomon's time. Then crossing the valley and passing by the Garden of Gethsemane, we went over the Mount of Olives to Bethany, doubtless in the same path our blessed Lord was wont to take. From the reputed house of Martha and Mary we proceeded to the cave called the Tomb of Lazarus, where as we sat by it I read aloud the deeply interesting scenes recorded in John xi. that there occurred.

We returned to the city, having previously arranged for a religious service in the large hall of our hotel, with the consent of the proprietor. It being the general wish that I should preach, the following sermon was delivered on that occasion. At eight o'clock, when our people at home were closing their morning services, we were assembled in that "upper room" on Mount Zion, very like those upper rooms where Jesus and his disciples were accustomed to meet in the same city. The sun's last rays had faded from the brow of Olivet, and he had gone down over the valley of Ajalon and the sea beyond.

That was a specially interesting religious assembly—about thirty of us, fellow-travelers, and strangers casually met, over twenty of whom were Americans, and others from England, Scotland and Ireland, all speaking the same language, and having a common Christian faith, though belonging to different denominations. A Presbyterian minister, Rev. R. R. Booth, of Connecticut, read the first hymn, and the Scriptures containing an account of our Lord's sufferings and death, and offered prayer. A Baptist minister from Massachusetts, Rev. W. C. Child, led the singing, and a clergyman of the Dutch Reformed church, Rev. R. B. Welch, from the State of New York, prayed at the close.

A window just back of my temporary pulpit opened upon the ancient Pool of Hezekiah. In front, at the eastern end of the room, another window overlooked the site of the Temple and the Mount of Olives. A near glance at the left brought Calvary to view. What an interesting spot for those who sympathized with Christ and His religion, to hold a service to His honor! We had been that day treading in His very footsteps, and beholding objects upon which He once looked. We had been along by the place of His sorrow and conflict in the Garden; where he was scourged and condemned in Pilate's Judgment Hall; where He bore His own cross up the hill Calvary till He fainted under it; where He was crucified, entombed and rose from the dead. And these places were all now near us, and Christ Himself seemed preciously near.

In thought and sympathy we were carried back to the time when these wonderful events transpired. Our Saviour was before us and with us, the chief among ten thousand and the One altogether lovely. He must be our theme—the theme of our songs, our Scripture lessons, our prayers, our preaching. What He was and is, what He had done and suffered for us, filled our thoughts and deeply affected our hearts. Any theme but Christ and Him crucified would have been out of place. The hymns we sung were: "All hail the power of Jesus' name," "When I survey the wondrous cross," and "Jerusalem, my happy home!" That precious Rest Day in the City of the Great King will long be remembered.

CHRIST ALONE.

Preached on Mount Zion in Jerusalem, Lord's Day, March 18, 1860.

Isaiah lxiii. 3.—I HAVE TRODDEN THE WINE-PRESS ALONE.

THE central truth of the Old Testament as well as of the New is the world's Redeemer—the cross of Christ. In the text with its connected passages, the prophet seems to have a vivid dramatic vision of the suffering, dying Saviour. He sees Him as He approaches the end of His mission. He hears His voice. He comprehends His all-important work as alone He drinks the cup of Gethsemane, and bears unaided the crushing burden of Calvary. He witnesses His steadfast endurance—His wondrous triumph. The bleeding Sufferer emerges from His tremendous trial and conflict a glorious Conqueror. He has passed through a scene and accomplished a work for which none was fitted but himself. He has trodden the wine-press alone. There are positions in the universe, in God's moral government, in the plan of Salvation, and in the sinner's heart, which Jesus only can fill. His person and character are peculiar and unique. Several particulars are readily suggested which present His place and office as solitary and indivisible.

I. *Christ was alone in personally undertaking the work of salvation.* It was God's purpose to make in this ruined world some of the brightest exhibitions of His benevolence, wisdom and power. Here, where Satan had succeeded in his temptations, where the human race had fallen, God determined to rear for Himself a kingdom which should finally prevail against the foe. Here where sin had abounded, grace should much more abound. Who could do this work, in view of the mighty obstacles to be overcome, the unparalleled outlay necessary, and the supreme exigencies it involved? Who is meet for the appointment, qualified for, or adequate to, the stupendous undertaking? Who can secure the pardon of the guilty, and yet abridge not the claims of the broken Law? Who can sustain the integrity of the Divine Government, and yet cancel the rebel's transgression? Who can open the door barred by infinite Justice, and let the prisoner go free? What being, though clothed with any one of the attributes of Jehovah, could effect the salvation of the lost. Mercy, heaven-descended angel, might pity and plead for them; but Mercy could never atone for their guilt. Love, the very essence of Deity, might earnestly desire to redeem them from death, and lift them up into life and liberty; but Love cannot annihilate Justice. Those to be saved are *sinners*, rightly condemned. The curse of the Law they have violated, so good and glorious in its nature and purpose, so solemn and awful in its sanctions and penalty, is resting on them like the weight of eternity. And that Law, like its Divine Author, is unchangeable: it cannot be abridged; it cannot be repealed. Who, then, can accomplish the required task, and harmonize Law and Justice in the redemption of sinful men? Oh Earth! canst thou furnish a Saviour? Can any one of the human race, were he the worthiest and most virtuous of all, do this great work? Alas! such an one himself must perish, unless this work be done for him. Unable to save himself, what can *he* do towards lifting *a world* up out of its condemnation? Heaven! hast thou an angel adequate to the task? Angels are dependent beings. In their various spheres they serve and glorify their Maker. This obligation limits their work. They cannot save even one of the fallen spirits, or rebel angels. How then can they achieve the world's redemption? They may earnestly desire to look into the great mystery and scan its wonders, but the work itself exceeds the utmost reach of their ability.

The birds sing their glad welcome to the life and loveliness of a vernal season; but they have no power to renew the face of the earth and cover it with beauty and bloom. So those immortal songsters of Paradise, the holy angels, may fill all heaven with joy when a sinner repents; but they never could produce the new creation over which they rejoice. Could God the Father, in His *absolute* character, do this work, without the mediation of His Son? As far as we know, there was but one Being in the universe—oh give thanks and be grateful for the One—who could render the world's salvation possible, and that was JESUS CHRIST. "Lo, I come," said He, "to do thy will, O God."

II. *Christ was alone in the Divine incarnation.* This sacred mystery was essential to the work of redemption. In this appears its wonderful adaptation, its astonishing efficacy. In "the fullness of time God sent forth His Son, made of a woman, made under the law." "In the beginning was the Word, and the Word was with God and the Word was God. And the Word was made flesh and dwelt among us." "Without controversy, great is the mystery of godliness: God was manifest in the flesh, justified in the Spirit, seen of angels, preached unto the Gentiles, believed on in the world, received up into glory."

Here is a fact of infinite interest and importance. Here is a truth, one of the most remarkable and marvelous in the whole compass of Revelation—the incarnation of Deity, the advent of Christ into our world, the Son of God born of the virgin Mary in yonder Bethlehem. This wonderful event stands by itself. Nothing in the universe is like it. Immanuel, God with us, becoming a helpless infant in the arms of a human mother, and passing through the various stages of an earthly existence. Amazing fact! Mystery of mysteries! Jehovah-Jesus,

> "From the highest throne of glory
> To the cross of deepest woe,
> Came to ransom guilty captives!—
> Flow my praise, forever flow!"

The almighty and glorious Creator, by whom and for whom are all things, made His abode with sinful men in the humblest walks of life.

This is a solitary instance. No being from another world has ever done the like. None has come from a distant sphere—from some pure star in the heavens—to make earth his home. Angels at different times and on special occasions, have visited our world; but they have never become its inhabitants. There is no record of one ever being born or having died on these mortal shores. We sometimes in our communings with God, in our thoughts and visions of Heaven, in a solemn nearness to death under the power of disease or at the departure of a dear friend, seem to linger a little on the confines of another world; but we have not yet entered its portal, nor breathed its immortal air, nor experienced its sublime reality. So angel messengers, feeling a deep and strange sympathy in our behalf, may be around and among us, but they are not of us; we are not linked to them by any ties of kindred. But God the Redeemer came nearer to us than they. He crossed the profound and awful chasm, caused by sin, that lay between the Divine and human. *"He took on Him the seed of Abraham,"* that He might grasp and encircle us in all the powerful sympathies of kindred and brotherhood. And oh, what treasures, what gifts of life and love, of hope and immortality, He brought with Him and laid at our feet!

Great men have appeared in different ages and at distant epochs, who have shed the light of their genius upon the world and by their deeds changed the current of its history. The heavens have opened at their glance, and in beautiful order have gathered into constellations, spheres and systems. The earth, summoned and questioned by science, has revealed her laws and disclosed her treasures. And mind itself, acquiring new vigor from its investigations, has ventured on flights and made discoveries, not only astonishing in themselves, but to-day affecting all the interests of the world's civilization. Confucius, in wisdom, towered above his countrymen like the princely oak in the forest. Socrates, rising superior to his age, seemed almost to break through into the region of Divine illumination. Calvin, in theological discrimination and statement, was an Alpine summit among his contemporaries. Newton, grasping some of the simplest laws of nature, was borne aloft to a grander survey of the system of the universe. Washington, in defence of human right and freedom, and as an example of moral virtue, patriotic devotion and self-sacrifice, stands forth in unparalleled grandeur. Yet these, in all their greatness, were only men. They were of the earth, earthy. But when JESUS appeared, " though found in fashion as a man," He was in reality " the Lord from heaven." And how does all science pale before His revealings of truth, life and immortality? When He spoke to man, what gleams of hope shot into the gloom of despair! Before His instructions, how the mists of error and the clouds of ignorance vanished away! He pointed to the skies, and disclosed a pathway to the glorious regions that lie beyond the stars! He planted the seeds of the great Banyan-tree of the gospel, which shall take root in every land, and whose branches, bending to the ground and rising to the sky, bathed in the light and vocal with the music of heaven, shall overshadow the whole earth.

Many distinguished men have been born into the world; but we see Jesus as the alone Godman. The Incarnation is an event that stands by itself in a unique and sublime isolation. And when we think of its design and our relation to it, how does it rise in greatness and value, and impress us by its infinite importance! Other events may engross attention for a season, but, in its bearings on human weal and destiny, this immeasurably surpasses them all. And its importance will increase. As earth fades and its vanities recede, as life wanes into the shadow of death, and the world to come draws near, with its certain judgment and everlasting awards, your relation to the Christ of God, the incarnate Redeemer, will tower into an interest that overshadows every thing else. Eternity will not be too long to lament your folly, if you have not availed yourselves of the gracious offer of salvation, nor too long to utter your grateful rejoicings if, with penitent and believing hearts accepting it, you have been made partakers of the Divine nature.

> "Dear Lord and Saviour! for thy gifts
> The world were poor in thanks, though every soul
> Were to do naught but breathe them, every blade
> Of grass, and every atomie of earth
> To utter them like dew."

III. *Christ was alone perfect in His human life, and essentially Divine in His ministrations.* In this two-fold nature He lived here humble and obedient as a creature, yet exercising the authority and power of the Creator. As God, He was the Author of the Law; as Man, He obeyed it to perfection. "He did no sin, neither was guile found in His mouth." Here He stands alone. Patriarchs and Prophets under the former dispensation, and Apostles and saints under the gospel, though eminent servants of God, and occupying by His appointment positions of great responsibility and usefulness, have not been free from imperfection and sin. Moses, with all his meekness and wisdom, sometimes erred. David, a man after God's own heart though he was, experienced the bitterness of repentance for his transgression. Paul and Barnabas, chosen servants of our Lord, separated from each other amid sharp contention. So imperfection attaches more or less to all human beings. The most Godly and sagacious are not free from sin. Not so with Jesus. No blemish was ever discovered in Him. No infirmities marred the resplendent integrity of His character. His example was perfect. Amid temptations and conflicts, privations and sorrows, misrepresentation and insult, calumny and cruelty, He never did a wrong act, indulged an evil thought, or contracted the least taint of impurity. Oh, what a treasure earth held in Him—a Being of sinless perfection!

Look at His ministrations—His works of mercy and of might. Here He is preëminent and alone, excelling all who have preceded and followed Him. Whether He opened His lips as a Teacher or commanded a miracle, "never man spake like this Man." We are astonished at the number and variety of His mighty works, some of them recorded, others only hinted at in the Gospel narratives. He controlled the elements of nature; exercised dominion over evil spirits; cured instantaneously prolonged and fatal diseases; and restored to life the dead and buried. Everywhere He scattered mercy and blessing, life and salvation. And all this supernatural energy and omnipotent power were inherent and original. In this respect He differed from other miracle-workers, whether prophets or apostles. To them superhuman power was delegated, and they exercised it through some instrumental object or in the Divine Name. The mighty deeds of Moses in Egypt are associated with the rod in his hand. He must stretch that wondrous staff over the Red Sea, and cast the branch into the bitter fountain of Marah, to see desired results. But Jesus has only to speak and will. "Be whole!" and health returns. "Arise!" and the sleeping dead awakes. "Come forth!" and the tomb gives back its trust. "Peace, be still!" and the tumultuous billows are calmed. Most convincingly He proved the assertion, "I am the Resurrection and the Life." And obedient wind and wave and storm recognized in Him their God. Apostles ascribed their miraculous power to Him. To the cripple at yonder Beautiful Gate they said: "In the name of Jesus of Nazareth, rise up and walk." But Christ said to those whom He healed: "*I* will, be thou clean; Thou deaf and dumb spirit, *I* charge thee to come out of him;" and to the dead son of the widow of Nain, "Young man, *I* say unto thee, arise!" Thus did the miracles of Jesus surpass all others, vindicating His Messiahship and symbolizing the future triumphs of the gospel.

IV. *Christ was alone in the nature of His sufferings and death.* Suffering is the result of sin. It follows the violation of law. Whoever sins against God, or against himself, *must* suffer. Our Lord taught this when He charged the impotent man whom He healed at Bethesda's pool, to sin no more, lest a worse thing come upon him. But our Lord's sufferings had no such origin. Intense as they were beyond all that mortal ever experienced or conceived, they were endured by a Being of spotless innocence. When He bowed under the agony of the Garden, and prayed that, if it were possible, that cup might pass from Him; when His soul was exceeding sorrowful, even unto death; that bloody baptism of anguish overwhelmed Him, not in consequence of any sin or guilt of His own. It was the hour and power of darkness, a terribly fierce and bitter conflict with Satan, and the crushing weight of a world's iniquities, whose awful pressure He sustained. It was the Innocent suffering, resisting, enduring for the guilty, that the guilty might escape eternal condemnation and wrath. It was the Divine Saviour, as a voluntary substitute for the sinner under the law, that He might become "the end of the law for righteousness to every one that believeth." "Surely He hath borne our griefs, and carried our sorrows." *He trod the wine-press alone.* "And the Lord hath laid on Him the iniquity of us all"—

> "That He who gave man's breath might know
> The very depths of human woe."

A skeptic once said: "Socrates died like a philosopher, but Jesus Christ like a God!" Ah! there is but one Calvary in the world, one cross of expiation, one vicarious Victim, one expiring Saviour whose blood is efficacious to atone for sin. The death of that Saviour stands out in the universe by itself in unparalleled sublimity and moral grandeur. That was the culminating point in the great Propitiation, the tremendous crisis where the hope of our race was centered and suspended. Oh, what a scene for earth and heaven to witness! There stood the Redeemer firm to His purpose, bearing up the burden of a condemned and dying world. And only Jesus could stand there.

Martyrs have died for their faith, patriots for their country, but there has been no death in our world like that of Christ. Were it possible for man to give a thousand lives, "None can by any means redeem his brother, or give to God a ransom for him." " But God commendeth His love toward us in that while we were yet sinners Christ died for us." When some men die benefits accrue to others. Places may be left for them to occupy, or wealth to possess. But there is no moral virtue in any human death. Could the touching lament of the heart-broken king have been realized—" Would God I had died for thee, Oh Absalom, my son, my son!"—it would not have availed for the rebellious soul. But from the death of Christ what benefits! It opened for the world a door of salvation. It bridged the gulf that separated man from God—earth from heaven. In that death Justice and Forgiveness blended, "Mercy and Truth met together, Righteousness and Peace kissed each other;" and so " God was in Christ reconciling the world unto Himself."

Jesus came into the world to die. That event was always before Him. He frequently alluded to it; He desired its fulfillment. " I have a baptism to be baptized with, and how am I straitened till it be accomplished." As it drew near and He saw it in all its dread and unutterable reality, He knew He must endure it *alone*. He had always had a few sympathizing disciples and friends, and the constant presence and aid of His Father. But now in the very darkest scene of trial and pain comes the heavy shadow of desertion. As the terrible tragedy proceeded, where were His disciples? " Of the people there was none with me." As the weight of the world's guilt rested upon Him in that dark and awful hour, under a sense of abandonment He exclaimed, "*My God, my God, why hast thou forsaken me?*" Was not this the supreme moment when He tasted death for those who otherwise in the outer gloom of the second death would have been forever separated from God? "He trod the winepress alone." He emerged from that scene of conflict and endurance a triumphant victor—man's great enemy conquered, and the world in possession of a finished redemption. His garments were dyed with the blood of atonement. In His wonderful resurrection, self-summoned and achieved, He appeared "glorious in His apparel, traveling in the greatness of His strength, speaking in righteousness, mighty to save."

Where shall we find a parallel to all this? Has another such scene anywhere transpired? Is another such fact lodged in any part of the universe? History! thou hoary chronicler of the past, unroll thy records, disclose their wonders, and search out all thou hast forgotten to write—wilt thou find another event like this? Prophet! that gazest down the ages to come, and seest all that is glorious and marvelous in the future—say, is it there? Ye worlds, that sweep the circle of the heavens, which of you has been the place where *God was manifest in the flesh?* Where in all your realms has a Saviour died? Affected, perhaps, by the influence of that death, restraining, saving, glorious—yet it transpired not with you! Oh earth, rebellious earth! how has Jehovah looked upon thee, and visited thee, and made thy one and only Golgotha the center of a system before which the stars in yonder canopy shall fade, and all material splendors vanish away!

V. *Christ is alone as an Intercessor and Mediator.* "For there is one God and one mediator between God and man, the man Christ Jesus." Since His triumphant ascension, He occupies the throne of intercession to mediate and plead in behalf of sinners. Only through Him may we have access to God and heaven. The services and ceremonials of the Jewish priesthood were superseded by the incoming of the Christian dispensation, with its more excellent ministry, wherein Jesus "is the Mediator of a better covenant, which was established upon better promises." Priestly orders and functions, sacerdotal sacrifices and ceremonies, founded on offices and rites of the Jewish economy, are like the employment of an obsolete agency that has fulfilled its purpose and been dismissed. It is as though a man, after the completion of his edifice, should insist on retaining as a part of the building, the scaffolding, the ropes and the ladders, which had once been needful and proper, but are now not only useless, but an incumbrance and blemish.

In the New Testament, believers, wherever found, "are an holy priesthood to offer up spiritual sacrifices, acceptable to God through Jesus Christ." They are to execute the commission or commands of the only Head and Lawgiver of the Christian church, and thus show forth the praises of Him who called them out of darkness into His marvelous light." Jesus is the High Priest of their profession, who is passed into the heavens, hath an unchangeable priesthood, and " is able to save them to the uttermost that come unto God by Him, seeing He ever liveth to make intercession for them." To Christ we must come directly and personally, in penitence and faith, and through His atoning merit find acceptance with God. Through other methods, whether of idolatry or superstition or ceremony, men are ever asking as did the Pharisees of Jesus, "What shall we do that we might work the works of God?" His reply was: "*This is the work of God, that ye believe in Him whom He hath sent.*" The only Mediator hath said: "I am the door; by me if any man enter in he shall be saved." "I am the way, the truth, and the life; no man cometh unto the Father but by me." Inspired Apostles have added: "Other foundation can no man lay than that is laid, which is Christ Jesus." "Neither is there salvation in any other; for there is none other name under heaven given among men, whereby we must be saved."

Such, brethren, is Jesus the Son of God, separate and singular in His character and position, as He appears in undertaking the work of salvation, in the incarnation, in His life and deeds, in His sufferings and death, in His mediation and intercession. Hence I observe :—

1. While Jesus is our only He is also our all-sufficient Saviour. Included among the lost whom He came to seek and save, when we see His adaptation to His great work, and realize our need, we feel that there is none but Christ. All our merits, works, hopes,—what are they without Him? Oh Jesus!

> "Should my zeal no respite know,
> Should my tears forever flow,
> All for sin could not atone,
> Thou must save, and thou alone."

What attributes, excellences, riches, unutterable attractions center in Christ! "Unto you therefore which believe, He is precious"—the "Chiefest among ten thousands, the ONE altogether lovely." He is our Life, our Hope, our Peace, our Joy. And we are complete in Him, in whom all fullness dwells; and "who of God is made unto us wisdom and righteousness and sanctification and redemption." He is all this to every believer of every name in every place. In gladness and gloom, in prosperity and adversity, in life and death, here and hereafter, He is their all-sufficient and eternal portion. Every renewed heart must breathe the grateful and adoring aspiration: "Whom have I in heaven but thee, and there is none upon earth that I desire besides thee."

2. If Jesus be the only Saviour, without faith in Him there is no salvation. A sinner out of Christ is a sinner lost. A world without the knowledge of Christ, is a world lying in darkness and the shadow of death. But "whosoever believeth on Him shall not perish, but have everlasting life." There must be something more than intelligence, refinement and wealth, splendid churches and gorgeous ceremonials, correct morals and even hearing and speaking the name of Jesus; there must be a personal apprehension and acceptance of Christ by faith, as a spiritual act of self-renunciation, trust, and submission to Him. To be saved is to have Christ in the heart and Christ in the life. He only is a true Christian who be-

lieves, and aims to live according to the gospel. That is only a true church whose members are regenerate, holding Christ as the Divine Head and sole Mediator and Intercessor before God. That only is a true ministry that preaches Christ as He is, as Apostles preached Him, Christ and Him crucified. Christ first, Christ last, Christ always, Christ alone. "God forbid that I should glory, save in the cross of our Lord Jesus Christ, by whom the world is crucified unto me, and I unto the world."

3. How great the guilt and condemnation of him who rejects the only Saviour! To despise, by indifference or otherwise, the Christ of God, to trample upon His mercy, and turn from the pleadings of His love, must insure an awful doom. "How shall we escape if we neglect so great salvation?" He that despised Moses' law died without mercy. How aggravated then will be the punishment of him who perishes under the gospel! Come, oh friend! to Jesus, your only Refuge! He has rendered your salvation possible—certain, if you believe. Reject Him—believe not—and your eternal ruin is inevitable. You must reap as you have sown!

4. How glorious the prospect of the believer in the one Saviour! They who are His in a life of faith, love and obedience, participate in His

unspeakable riches. The glory of their salvation is in proportion to the greatness of the sacrifice that secured it. All things are theirs, life, death, the present, the future. What promises to cheer and support; what a perpetual Comforter and Guide; what companionship, safety, joys, songs, by the way; what mansions prepared in heaven; what hope in the coming of the Lord! "They shall be mine, saith the Lord of hosts in that day when I make up my jewels." That day—the final day—fast approaches. Its highest glory will consist—not in its unparalleled scenes and attending events; the vast and shining array of accompanying angels, the dazzling splendors of the great white throne, the sound of the Archangel's trumpet waking all the dead, the stupendous exhibition of power in the resurrection, the wrapping of earth in a sheet of flame, and rolling the heavens together as a scroll—not in any or all these will the Son of God find His highest and peculiar honors; but rather in His ransomed people; for *"He will come to be glorified in His saints, and to be admired in all them that believe."*

We know much of Jesus in this world. We are united to Him by faith and love. His presence and blessing are with us. And as we linger in the places where He lived and taught and suffered and died, how near to us He seems!

But the day cometh when we shall see face to face and know as we are known. "When Christ who is our life shall appear, then shall we also appear with Him in glory." Oh, in that day, free from sin and imperfection, we shall see in the Great Propitiation exhaustless treasures and enrapturing glories. Our eyes will rest on new attractions at Bethlehem. We shall see Nazareth beaming as in the glory of a transfiguration, and Tabor's height shining as the mount of God. The lake of Galilee will be transparent and luminous as the sea of glass. Our undying interest in Gethsemane will grow deeper and more intense. Calvary will rise and bloom and brighten in its sublimest manifestation of Divine Love. The tomb where Jesus lay and whence He rose triumphant will seem radiant as the gate of Paradise, and Olivet's summit of ascension will be crowned with a golden sunlight not of earth. Though these places that we visit and look upon now with such profound interest, as literal localities may be changed, yet in their spiritual significance as connected with the great truths of our religion, they will remain forever, and as we comtenplate our interests associated therewith, from the serene heights of immortality, all our admiration of their value and glory will center in CHRIST ALONE!

GETHSEMANE.

Ye shall be scattered every man to his own, and shall leave me alone.—JOHN XVI. 32.

WITHIN the olive shade
   The Saviour see,
As there he knelt and prayed,
   My soul, for thee;
While cold and damp midnight,
Pale moon and dim starlight
Beheld thy strange sad sight,
   Gethsemane!

Even the faithful fail
   Vigils to keep;
They sink behind the vail
   Of weary sleep.
Jesus is left alone,
Bowed on dank earth and stone,
And thou dost hear his moan,
   Gethsemane!

Why is my Saviour there,
    In sighs and fears,
Under a burdening prayer,
    In cries and tears?
While sorrow's dread control
O'erwhelms his holy soul,
His blood to thee doth roll,
    Gethsemane!

He took the bitter cup
    His Father gave;
Resigned, he drank it up,
    My soul to save:
Man's guilt and Satan's hate,
Heart-crushing load so great,
How death-like was its weight,
    Gethsemane!

Garden of love and woe,
    How dear to me!
I oft in spirit go,
    Jesus to see,
Who gives me heavenly aid
To pray as there he prayed,
Within thy sacred shade,
    Gethsemane!

OLIVE-TREES IN GETHSEMANE.

SERMON VI.

THE LORD OUR HOME.

———

New Haven, Conn.

PREFATORY NOTES.

SOON after my return home from nearly a year's tour in Europe and the East, the following sermon was preached. In a previous discourse I had given some account of my observations abroad and my happiness in again meeting my people and friends, as they thronged the sanctuary to welcome me back. But this sermon seems now the more suitable to be included in this series.

After the service held on Mount Zion, mentioned in the last "Notes," we enjoyed other Rest Days of wonderful interest with precious services in Jerusalem, at the Sea of Galilee, and at Beirût. After leaving the last place our steamer stopped and gave us several hours on the islands of Cyprus and Rhodes, and we passed in full view of Patmos. We stayed a day at Smyrna, three or four at Constantinople, and another at Athens where, on Mars' Hill to over twenty fellow-travelers, I read Paul's address, (Acts xvii. 22–31) standing where he stood, with some of the same temples in view that met his eye. We made a short visit to France and England, and I heard Mr. Spurgeon preach again in London. Taking the American Steamship Adriatic at Southampton, we had a successful homeward voyage.

THE LORD OUR HOME.

Preached in the First Baptist Church, New Haven, Conn., June 3, 1860.

Psalm xc. 1.—LORD, THOU HAST BEEN OUR DWELLING-PLACE IN ALL GENERATIONS.

WHAT a sweetly-cherished, ever-inspiring thought is HOME, to the wanderer in distant lands! A blessed realization at his return, he looks again into the faces of loved ones, and finds refuge and rest in the one spot dearer than all the world. The text is a peculiar expression of the devout soul finding in the Lord Himself what is most attractive and precious in our domestic life. This beautiful and sublime Psalm, sounding like a solemn chant of hope and immortality along the aisles and arches of some old charnel-house, is styled, "A prayer of Moses, the man of God." One of the oldest of the Psalms, it is supposed to have been written in the wilderness about the time the spies brought back an evil report of the land of Canaan. Then the period of human life was shortened. Then the Israelites were adjudged to a forty years' pilgrimage of tent-life, and to die in their wanderings. The actual "dying out of the older generation on account of their transgressions, and the threatened exclusion of Moses himself from the Promised Land, were exactly suited to produce such views of man's mortality and sinfulness as are here presented, but without destroying the anticipation of a bright futurity, such as really ensued upon the death of Moses, and is prospectively disclosed in the conclusion of this Psalm." How appropriately then does the meek man of God look up from such a scene as was before him of painful journeyings, of transient tents, of sinful complainings, of pestilence and death, with a prayer toward heaven: "Lord, thou hast been our dwelling-place in all generations." The term *dwelling-place* contains exactly our idea of *home*, by which we denote the center of our domestic life and affections. Dr. J. A. Alexander renders the passage, "Lord, a home hast thou been to us, in generation and generation." I love to think of God as my Creator, Preserver, Benefactor—my Father and Friend; but there is something peculiarly sweet and blessed in the thought of His being my *home*, my dearest and most cherished dwelling-place.

Let us take hold of this idea and make it for a little time the subject of our meditations.

THE LORD OUR HOME! Is it not inspiring, precious, glorious, to rise up to the apprehension, the possession, the enjoyment of such a wonderful reality?

One of the first things associated with a home is that mentioned in the text, a PLACE OF DWELLING, a SHELTER or REFUGE—a spot where one can be enclosed and protected. The pioneer who goes out into the great forest or upon the wide prairie to obtain lands to subdue and cultivate, engages his earliest care to secure a shelter for himself. He must have a home even if it be a rude cabin hasty in construction and uncouth in appearance. Wild beasts may have their haunts about him, and he needs a protection from them. Storms may come gloomily and rage fiercely over his head, and he must have a retreat from them. Night, with its damp dews and chill airs, settles upon him, and he must have a covert from its darkness and ills. How utterly desolate and exposed his life without a home refuge! The traveler in foreign lands and the pilgrim who wanders on the desert, as each day comes to a close, seek some protection of roof and walls, tent or cave, which for the time shall be as a home and hiding-place from exposure and danger. The family group and even the lonely individual make it one of their first objects to have a dwelling-place. And thus in the hours of relaxation and toil, as in the hours of darkness and tempest, they find both a retreat and defense. Think of the tourist amid Alpine summits, and no friendly hospice at night-fall. Think of the desert wanderer lying down in the darkness where the robber or the wild-beast may prey upon him. Think of a family group of delicate women and tender children, without a roof, canopy or protecting wall to shield them from pitiless storms and biting cold. Yes, there is something indescribably sweet and refreshing in the kindly shelter of a home. We know how in some measure to appreciate and prize it.

Now let us apply this to the blessed idea in the text. The Lord our home, and as such a sheltering refuge for us. And in Him what strength of roof, what thickness of walls, what certainty of protection and defense that shelter has! That home is a castle as well—a strong tower into which the righteous run and are safe. All over Europe are found grand old castles, vast in proportions, strong in construction, and surmounted with lofty towers. These were the homes of men in feudal times. There they were protected from hostile clans and kingdoms. But God is a refuge for us, a stronghold from the enemy. What a blessed shelter the trusting soul finds in Him! And how much we need such a home! Wanderers we all are, away from our Father's house—away from the home circle of original purity and love. All we like sheep have gone astray. We have broken from the fold, scorned its protection, refused its safety. We seek, we find, we make, we inhabit earthly homes. However humble we prize them and enjoy their shelter. But what can they do to protect and save the soul, that more than the body needs a refuge? Satan smiles at castle walls, and Death laughs at bolts and bars. Oh, soul! where is thy shelter? Out on the deserts of sin, a far wanderer from heaven, in regions swept by wrath-storms, and pierced by divine thunderbolts, where death-vapors fill the air, and fearful foes lurk by every path; how and where wilt thou find a safe retreat, a welcome home? In God alone; in the Good Shepherd, who came to seek and to save the lost. Hearing His call, obeying His voice, putting thy hand in His, thou art led back to thy Father's house; there thou dost find a blessed home; there thou art sheltered and safe. The Lord is thy tabernacle, and His pillar of cloud and fire is with thee. "Let storms of woe in whirlwinds rise," let dangers thicken, let sin accuse, and Satan throw his darts, let every human expectation perish, and let even thine earthly house be dissolved:

> "Let sorrow's rudest tempest blow,
>   Each cord on earth to sever,
> Our King says come, and there's our home
>   Forever, oh, forever!"

Another idea associated with home is that of REPOSE, QUIETUDE, REST. Weariness and lassitude, drooping vigor and the failure of elasticity of life and limb, we have all more or less experienced. Labor at length becomes painful, journeying and sight-seeing exhaust one's strength, excitement prolonged is burdensome, and even pleasure-hunting becomes tiresome. Beyond a brief period of exertion or physical toil, the idea of rest becomes a powerful desire and a sweet anticipation. The workingman, whether he employ hand, head, or foot, body or mind, turns not only his thoughts but his steps toward home as a place of repose. There he forgets his toils, throws off his cares, and finds refreshing quiet, and a renewal of his strength. The traveler over the grand passes of the Alps thinks of the inn or hospice that his weary feet will reach as the shadows darken. The pilgrim in the East longs for the tree-shade or rock-shade where he may rest a little from the burning noon-day sun, and rejoices in the tent-cover under which he may repose at night. And beyond these he looks wistfully to the dear home in the land he has left, and earnestly covets its rest again. The journeying Israelites in their desponding hours looked back to their dwelling-place in Egypt, and in their hopeful moments forward to the promised rest. And when they thought of the burdens and sorrows of the one, and how for their sins and unbelief they must be denied an entrance to the other, where could they look, where could Moses the man of God look, but upward, and with the blessed assurance of the text? "Lord, thou hast been our dwelling-place in all generations." In thee we find a home. There, brethren, we look. There is our repose. There is the "Rock of ages cleft for me." There are the wings under whose shadow I trust. There are the everlasting arms on which I recline. There is the hiding-place to which I fly. Looking there I say, "Return unto thy rest, oh my soul." He who is a stranger to that dwelling-place, is virtually without a home. Like Noah's dove over the wide waste of flood-waters, he has no place to rest.

We remember the days of impenitence and the hours of religious conviction, when we felt our isolation from God, and had a consciousness of being wretched wanderers, restless and forlorn, without a home or refuge. Our mournful cry was,—

> "Oh, where shall rest be found,
> Rest for the weary soul?"

Ah! it is the *soul*, outside the walls of salvation, wandering on the plains of sin, or stumbling on the dark mountains of death, that most of all needs a home. But like the evil spirits that range over dry places seeking rest and finding none, it never enters a safe refuge, it never finds true repose, till it hears and obeys the sweet inviting and commanding voice of Jesus: "Come unto me all ye that labor and are heavy laden, and I will give you rest." Here it is that we leave the restless, houseless, shelterless region of impenitence and sin, and enter the gates of righteousness which the Lord in infinite mercy opens to us. Here in this new dwelling-place, beautiful, wonderful, sublime, the eye is delighted, and the heart is satisfied, and the whole being finds a heavenly quiet. Glorious habitation! the soul that rests in thee may with the prophet, "Call thy walls Salvation and thy gates Praise." We value the spot that has given us rest for the night, that has shielded us from the prowling thief or hungry beast. We prize the quiet of our homes, where wearied toil lies down, and wasted energies recuperate. But there is no rest so sweet, so blessed, so safe, so life-renewing as the soul finds when it comes home to God. As soul-weariness, soul-labor and soul-burdens, before the weight of sin and guilt is thrown off, are the most crushing and grievous, so the rest found in the Lord of life and salvation, is the most sweet and refreshing. Oh, blessed dwelling-place! Happy are they whose home is there, whose rest is under the wings divine!

> "They who have made their refuge God
> Shall find a most secure abode;
> Shall walk all day beneath His shade,
> And there at night shall rest their head."

Another and the crowning element of home is AFFECTION, pervading, binding, sweetening all its interests. LOVE is the life, glory and atmosphere of home. Friends, associates, classmates, fellow-travelers may form strong attachments, may rejoice in pleasant ties of friendship, and delight in their subsequent renewals. But this can scarcely be called love. It is a glimmer of sunlight on the landscape, but not the dear warm hearth-fire of home; not the blessed blending of affections and sweet union of hearts that are the beauty and crown of the domestic circle. Love in its purest and most sacred forms lives and reigns in the home it has made, in the dwelling-place it has furnished and adorned. "God setteth the solitary in families," creating the pure, strong and tender ties of wedded, parental and filial affection. Around the family home, as the great and loving Father designed it, what sweet sympathies and heavenly associations cluster! What a sanctuary of love! What a type of Paradise! It is a beautiful spot, like an Eden before the curse came; like a garden where all choice, radiant and fragrant flowers spring up and blossom; over which softest and balmiest breezes float, laden with celestial aroma; where friendliest sunbeams delight to linger, and warm even the dull sod into life; where most musical birds sing all day long in the tree-tops, and the forms of guardian angels seem to flit in the evening moonbeams, while Jehovah's blessed banner of love is a sweet and sheltering canopy over the whole scene. Happy are they all, old and young, who have in this world such a dwelling-place—such a hallowed home where the purest and best of human affections find their appropriate and congenial objects, and their true and harmonious development. Temporary separations may occur; wide seas and distant lands may intervene; here business calls, and there study invites; but the true and loving heart is turning ever to the one cherished place and center of attraction dearer than every other.

Lord, a *home* hast thou been to us. Is it not delightful *thus* to think of Him? and to feel that in coming to Him we come to our Father's house, and are welcomed to the infinite riches of His loving heart? Thought is inadequate and language impotent to set forth the love that reigns in that home where God is the Father reverenced and obeyed with filial affection. Oh, the privilege of such a home, and how much we need it! Under the most favored circumstances with regard to this world, what wandering, desolate, houseless fugitives our souls are that have no dwelling-place of love in God! This wretched and unloving state of orphanage may not always be perceived; indeed, one may think little about it, until there comes a famine of earthly pleasures, and like the prodigal son he begins to be in want, and comes to himself and sees the wretchedness of his condition, and thinks of his Father's house with its abundant supplies. But he does not and cannot know of the fullness of the love that dwells there, that waits to welcome him there, that he himself may share and enjoy on his return hither. But he begins to realize it when, notwithstanding all his unworthiness and dreadful guilt, his Father comes a great way to meet him, falls on his neck and kisses him, in place of his tattered garments clothes him with the best robe, puts a ring upon his finger and shoes upon his bare and bruised feet, makes for him a special and sumptuous feast enlivening his whole house with joy, and receives him with a depth of affection that welcomes the lost as found and the dead as alive again. What a beautiful illustration of that dwelling-place or home of love into which the converted soul comes! Blessed home! Happy day that brought me to thy threshold, and within thy gates, and to the society and fellowship of the ransomed family! Is not this your experience, believing soul? Once a lost wanderer, unsatisfied and desolate, but now in mercy found and brought home to your Father's house and love! Ay, I hear you sing:

> "No more a wayward child,
>   I seek no more to roam,
> I love my heavenly Father's voice,
>   I love, I love His home."

Conscious of the meagerness of my attempts to set forth this rich theme, I wish I could make it so attractive that you all, every one, would be induced to find by blessed experience this home in the Lord; that the tottering feet of the aged would go up to its threshold and be welcomed in by the good angels standing there; that those whose tread is yet firm and strong would feel that they need a refuge there, and secure it now ere their feet shall slide; that those whose elastic step is ever bearing them away from the kind paternal roof, would turn and fly thither as clouds and doves to their windows; and that the patter of the dear children's feet might be heard going through its gates at the call of the Good Shepherd there.

Among the BENEFITS OF THIS HOME, besides the refuge it supplies, the repose it gives, and the love that pervades it, think of the *purity* of its atmosphere and surroundings. There is no deadly contagion there, no destroying malaria in the air, no poisonous plants grow upon those grounds, no polluting thing is to be feared. Those dwelling there have been cleansed in Life's flowing fountain; their robes have been washed and made white in the blood of the Lamb. Their hearts have all been made new. Oh, blessed home! how unlike all else is this world! All else in this world bears the taint of sin. What evil communications meet us—what corrupt manners abound! To what impure and fatal associations, and to what fearful paths and terrible dooms are the wanderers from God exposed! How they fall into the horrible pit and sink into the miry clay! But those in the household of faith are lifted above such perils. Delivered from the body of death, the old and unrenewed man with his deeds is put off, and the new man put on created after the image of Christ in knowledge and true holiness. There is a beauty of holiness that transcends all other beauty; and this is the characteristic of those whose home is in God, and whose manhood finds its pattern in the Lord Jesus. Many a soul, conscious of its guilt and unfitness for holy associations, and of its wretched orphanage and distance from heaven, has in the method of grace in the gospel, been brought home and made a beloved child, pure, loving and joyful in the family of God. Sweet and blessed home! Its portals are still open, and penitent souls are welcomed to its happy and heavenly associations.

Think, again, of the *peace* that abounds in this home. The world is full of commotion, strifes, vexations, and all sorts of jarring interests. There may be a tranquil place here, and a little sheltered spot there, like a land-locked harbor or mountain vale, where clashing elements rage not; but even there the soul needs the peace that Jesus gives, or its hours of unrest and anxious foreboding will not be few. Ah! there is no soul-peace, no serene and hopeful calm for the mind, till it can say of the Lord, "Thou art my dwelling-place." There is found that perfect peace that casts out fear, that fortifies while it soothes and rejoices the soul.

Storms often sweep along the mountains, rage in the valleys, and desolate the plains. Dark clouds frown in the sky, obscure the heavens, and send forth in terrible commotions their lightnings and thunders. But above these storms and clouds all is tranquil and serene. The air is pure and unvexed. The breezes are bland and refreshing. The sun shines in a clear and smiling sky. And around some mountain-top there, the birds flit, and sing their sweet melodies, and the tender flowers brighten and rejoice in the placid glory of their high abode. So is it with those who have come up to the heights of a divine love and faith, and have the Lord for their home. They dwell on high; the munition of rocks is their defense; they bask in the sunlight of Jesus' presence, and enjoy the heavenly peace He gives.

Think, finally, of the *permanence* of the blessings and privileges of this home. "Lord, thou hast been our dwelling-place in all generations." This world has its pleasures. Men seek and enjoy them. A certain happiness is found in various pursuits and stations. There is many a pleasant home where sympathy and love dwell, where different attractions and clustering interests render such a home delightful, and for a time it may seem that nothing is wanting to complete its joy. But in all this there is nothing permanent. Time soon works its changes. Sickness and death come. The dearest circles are broken up. These earthly enjoyments are scattered and lost. Oh, then, how the soul needs a *permanent* home—attachments that nothing can weaken or destroy—treasures that neither time nor death can affect. Well, here they are in this Divine dwelling-place—the Lord our Home—giving us shelter, rest and love, that are ours continually and forever, bringing us into pure, holy and heavenly associations, enthroning a sweet and sacred peace in our minds that no adversities can shake or destroy, and making all our real blessings and joys and treasures permanent in every change of time or place, secure from the ravages of death, and enduring with us and for us through the endless ages of eternity!

Oh, what a glorious home! Brother! thou that hast ever come into the household, and known the Lord thy refuge, thou wilt not, canst not leave it for aught the world can give. And poor homeless soul, far from thy Father's house, here is hope and salvation for thee. Stay not where thou art. Arise, and go to Jesus this very hour, and see how and with what joy to thee and to angels He will welcome thee home!

THE HEART'S HOME.

God is love; and he that dwelleth in love dwelleth in God, and God in him.—I John iv. 16.

O Lord, in whom are all my springs,
    Joyful to thee I come;
My grateful heart exultant sings
    To know thou art its home.

The shelter of thy glorious arms,
    How strong and safe and sweet!
From sense and sin, from all alarms,
    I fly to this retreat.

There is my sure and tranquil rest,
    In every troubled hour;
Weary, I lean upon thy breast,
    And feel its soothing power.

In that dear place of purest love,
    What wings encircle me!
Naught in the world can ever move
    My trusting soul from thee.

My Lord! if now I find in thee
    So blest and sweet a home,
What shall the heavenly mansion be
    When to its door I come?

INTERIOR OF THE CHURCH.

SERMON VII.

OPPOSITE SIDES OF THE PILLAR OF CLOUD.

Edinburgh, Scotland.

PREFATORY NOTES.

IN order to make my book a little larger and give more variety to its contents, I add the following sermons preached during my second tour abroad.

The Atlantic voyage being completed, I proceeded at once from Liverpool to the beautiful city of Edinburgh, finding a congenial home with those dear friends, Mr. T. G. Douglas and family. I was soon called upon by a deacon of the Parish Church in that vicinity, and invited to preach the next Sunday morning in the absence of the pastor, Rev. J. M. Lang, who was then on a visit to the United States. As the time arrived, the deacon met me in the vestry, and brought the gown and bands belonging to the pastor that I might be arrayed according to the custom for the pulpit. The gown fitted well, but while trying to adjust the bands I asked if it were necessary to wear them, and found that if I did not, the people would think I was an unordained minister, since only licentiates omit them. The congregation was large and attentive, all seeming to join in the singing and prayers and Scripture lessons, being well supplied with Bibles and hymn-books.

In the afternoon and evening I worshiped with the Dublin-St. Baptist church, it being the anniversary of the opening of their chapel, which they celebrate each year, engaging distinguished preachers. Rev. Alexander Maclaren of Manchester preached in the morning and evening and Dr. W. Lindsay Alexander of Edinburgh preached in the afternoon. I was glad of an opportunity to hear them. The sermon in the evening to a crowded house, was one of rare excellence and power, fully up to the great reputation of the preacher. At the close of the afternoon service, Deacon Rose took us—Dr. S. Graves and myself—to his delightful home to dine in company with Dr Alexander, who is quite as genial as he is ample physically and intellectually.

The next Sabbath morning I preached in this chapel on invitation of the venerable pastor, Rev. J. Watson, and his associate, Rev. Mr. Newnam. In the evening I heard the latter preach an excellent sermon. On another Lord's Day I heard in his own church with great pleasure Dr. H. Bonar whose sweet hymns we often sing.

OPPOSITE SIDES OF THE PILLAR OF CLOUD.

Preached in the National Presbyterian Church, Morningside. Edinburgh, Scotland, Sabbath, June 23, 1872.

Exodus xiv. 20.—IT CAME BETWEEN THE CAMP OF THE EGYPTIANS AND THE CAMP OF ISRAEL; AND IT WAS A CLOUD AND DARKNESS TO THEM, BUT IT GAVE LIGHT BY NIGHT TO THESE.

YOU have often noticed that Egypt and the Egyptians are set forth in the Scriptures as typical of an unregenerate condition, or of those who refuse to worship the true God. On the other hand the Chosen People, the subjects of the grand exodus, symbolize in every age the true servants of Jehovah. The two classes are in the world together. But the one hears the voice that calls and recognizes the hand that delivers them from the bondage of sin, and leads them to the better land. The other remains where they are, not careful to interpret aright and obey the Divine manifestations. It is remarkable how this sharply-defined difference among men still exists. Here the problem of life has its solution. We are, we do, we shall be, according as we arrange ourselves with reference to God, in the disclosures He makes to us. And things will be dark or light, obscure or clear, glorious or otherwise, from the position in which we are found. If we assume and maintain a wrong position, there will be nothing but darkness, obscurity and doom. But if we listen to and obey the Divine voice, we shall live and walk and dwell in the light and smile of our Heavenly Father's face.

The Chosen People had begun their march. They had reached the shore of the Red Sea. The mysterious Pillar of Cloud and Fire, the constant and most significant token of the Divine presence and guidance, went before them, hanging from the heavens in supernatural and sublime splendor. What more striking evidence could they have that God was with them, leading and defending them? They had not the Scriptures nor the experience of the ages that we have. They needed this wonderful Pillar, and God provided it for them. The Angel of God was in it, the Angel of the Covenant, the same that was afterward made flesh and dwelt among men,—our Saviour and Guide. At the margin of the Sea, the deep before them, and their foes pressing upon them behind, the Israelites were in a critical state; but the Divine resources are adequate to every emergency. It was at this point that the Angel of God and the Pillar of Cloud, which had gone before them, changed to their rear; and in the words of the text, "it came between the camp of the Egyptians and the camp of Israel; and it was a cloud and darkness to them, but it gave light by night to these." What was a light and guide to God's people was darkness and confusion to His enemies. So the one made the passage safely, and sang the song of triumph, and the other suffered defeat and miserably perished. The one, in accord with the Divine will, found light and help in the night of peril and trial. The other, opposed to that will, found what should have been light to them, if in the right, augmenting darkness deepening into doom. Here is the idea, the great truth, the impressive lesson, which the text flashes upon us. To the servants of God, to those who trust in Him, with loving, obedient hearts, who would ever know and do His will, a heavenly light shines; and the most difficult problems and experiences of life have a deep and precious meaning and generally a clear and satisfactory solution. But to those who disregard God, who do not set Him before them as the object of their highest reverance and love, these same problems and experiences are dark, cheerless, disappointing; a tangled economy without significance, satisfaction or hope. To the one the great Power and Wisdom, ordering all things, is light and guidance; to the other, it is a cloud and darkness. This is true in the survey of the Bible, of nature, of providence, of the purpose of life, of death and eternity. Let us delay a little upon each of these.

I. THE WORD OF GOD. The Bible is a book for the eye of faith, for the appreciation of a renewed heart—food for a spiritually-illumined mind. It makes all the difference in the world from what stand-point you view it or accept it. If you take your position at Calvary—as a penitent believer at the foot of the cross—and in the light that flashes from the atonement, read and understand the Scriptures, enlightened by the Spirit that dictated them, they gleam as matchless pearls of truth. They are divinely inspired messages. There is a unity and a glory in them that fill and thrill the soul. Their history is the history of redemption. Their prophecies are of the coming and establishment of the gracious kingdom. Their fulfillment in the New Testament is the complement and confirmation of the

Old. Every promise has its pledge; every invitation its endorsement; every revelation its reality. God's truth is the mirror of the human soul. It discloses its sad condition and deepest want. It brings to view also all that the soul needs to renovate and restore it and make it divine and Godlike. It opens to it a home of safety, where it may rest and feast and dwell. It lets it into gardens where purest fountains flow, all wholesome and delicious fruits are found, and sweetest songs of birds delight the ear. To Christian faith and experience the Bible is the light of God. It reveals Him on the throne, infinitely wise and good. The feeblest of His children is cared for and safe. It makes this life a school for heaven, and every severe lesson, every intricate problem, is a discipline and preparation for the future and better life. To the new-born soul, the Bible is a new book; God's light shining into the heart and unfolding His gracious purposes; a lantern in the hand of Jesus leading His follower safely and joyously onward to the world of glory. With this light shining upon them, the saints can go through every Red sea and wilderness in their path to heaven, and shout the victory on the farther shore.

But this book, so bright and guiding to God's people, is a cloud and darkness to His persistent enemies. They view it from the sinful, earthly, Egyptian side. They are not in sympathy with it, and do not comprehend it. The natural man cannot discern the things of the Spirit. Instead of coming to God through the Bible, the only medium in which He is truly or clearly seen, many thrust into His face their oppositions of science falsely so called, their philosophy and vain deceit, darkening counsel by their many words, and by their theories making confusion worse confounded. No wonder the Bible is dark to those who will not receive the light of God, and who reject the truth as it is in Jesus. They are with the Egyptians and not with the Chosen People. All true science and true philosophy will be in harmony with God and His word, and will find their highest and best interpretation there. But to stand in opposition to God, His revelation will be as cloud and darkness. It will be Sinai without Calvary; winter with no summer; night with no day; wrath without mercy; sin without redemption; and death without life. The Bible is a dark book to those who have no sympathy with its profound spiritual truths, and no reverential love toward its Divine Author.

> To faithless souls Heaven's clear and guiding light
> Is lost in cloud and ever-darkening night.

II. THE WORKS OF GOD—NATURE—OR GOD'S MANIFESTATION OF HIMSELF IN HIS CREATION. They· are like the Pillar between the two camps. The devout, joyous believer interprets Nature in its appearance, language and voice, very differently from the unbeliever. The one everywhere sees with delight the presence, providence, wisdom and power of God. These, pervading all nature, give beauty and glory to the grandest and minutest scenes and objects. The skeptic may have an appreciation of the beautiful and sublime in the material creation, but if he does not see a personal and infinite God in them to love and adore and trust in, he fails of the highest enjoyment. The brightest adorning of the outward world and the calm face of heaven, and the sweetest loveliness of the Creator's works, so radiant with the Divine glory, are as cloud and darkness to him. If you stand outside some grand religious temple and look at its exquisitely stained and figured windows, you see nothing but dull, blurred and indistinct enameling. But, when you enter the building, how clear and beautiful the colors appear in the light! So is it in the temple of God's creation. Study nature, with no reference to light pouring through it from God, but for itself alone, there is nothing better seen than the mere material enameling.

But stand within, a true worshiper of God, and the soul, looking up to the light, not only beholds the beautiful forms and colors, but understands their meaning and symbolism. Where the unbeliever sees in nature nothing but outward forms and various combinations of matter, the believer observes in every hill a Calvary or an Olivet; every mountain a Sinai or Tabor; every brook or river is a reminder of the stream that makes glad the city of God; and the starry garden of the skies is filled with budding hopes of immortality. The thoughts of God are revealed to us in the book of nature. As Spurgeon says, In the thunder and lightning, His grand and terrible thoughts; in the sunshine and the breeze, His loving and tender thoughts; in waving harvests, His careful and bounteous thoughts; from mountain-top and valley, His brilliant thoughts; and from the flowers that blossom at our feet, His sweet, pleasant, beautiful thoughts. Does the unrenewed heart perceive or enjoy them?

Let me give you a fine passage from one though a pantheist, yet a most careful observer of nature. "All things," he says, "are engaged in writing their history. The planet, the pebble, goes attended by its shadow. The rolling rock leaves its scratches on the mountain; the river, its channel in the soil; the animal, its bones in the stratum; the fern and leaf, their modest epitaph in the coal. The falling drop makes its sculpture in the sand or the stone. Not a foot steps into the snow or along the ground, but prints, in characters more or less lasting, a map of its march. Every act of the man inscribes itself in the memories of its fellows, and in his own manners and face. The air is full of sounds, the sky of tokens, the ground is all memoranda and signatures, and every object covered over with hints, which speak to the intelligent." This is beautiful and suggestive; but as the author rejects Christ and Divine Revelation, he sees no loving Father, and no symbol of Divine mercy, no lesson of salvation. As to these, all is cloud and darkness.

Let me now give you a passage from a Christian's standpoint, and see what light breaks forth to devout souls from things about us. "What wonderful provision God has made for us, spreading out the Bible into types of nature! What if every part of your house should begin to repeat the truths which have been committed to its symbolism!—the lowest stone would say, in silence of night, 'Other foundation can no man lay.' The corner-stone would catch the word, 'Christ is the corner-stone.' The taper burning by your bedside would stream up a moment to tell you, 'Christ is the light of the world.' If you gaze upon your children, they reflect from their sweetly sleeping faces the words of Christ, 'Except ye become as little children.' If, waking, you look towards your parents' couch, from that sacred place God calls Himself your Father and your Mother. Disturbed by the crying of your children, who are afflicted in a dream, you rise to soothe them, and hear God saying, 'So will I wipe away all tears from your eyes in heaven.' Returning to your bed, you look from the window. Every star hails you, but, chiefest, 'the Bright and Morning Star.' By and by flaming from the East, the flood of morning bathes your dwelling, and calls you forth to the cares of the day; and then you remember that God is the Lord, and that heaven is bright with His presence. Drawn by hunger you approach the table. The loaf whispers as you break it, 'Broken for you;' and the wheat of the loaf sighs, 'Bruised and ground for you.' The water that quenches your thirst says, 'I am the water of life.' If you wash your hands you can but remember the teachings of spiritual purity. If you wash your feet, that hath been done sacredly by Christ as a memorial. The very roof of your dwelling hath its utterance, and bids you look for the day when God's house shall receive its top stone. Go forth to your labor, and what thing can you see that hath not its message? The ground is full of sympathy. The flowers have been printed with teachings. The trees that only seem to shake their leaves with sport, are framing divine sentences. The birds tell of heaven, with their love-warblings in the green twilight. The sparrow is a preacher of truth. The hen clucks, and broods her chickens, unconscious, that, to the end of the world, she is part and parcel of a revelation of God to man. The sheep that bleat in the pastures, the hungry wolves that blink in the forest, the serpent that glides noiselessly in the grass, the raven that flies heavily across the field, the lily over which his shadow passes, the plough, the sickle, the wain, the barn, the flail, the threshing-floor,—all of them are consecrated priests, unrobed teachers, revelators, that see no vision themselves, but that bring to us thoughts of truth, contentment, hope, and love. All are ministers of God. The whole earth doth praise Him, and show forth His glory."

III. God's Providential dealings with His creatures. They are like the Pillar of Cloud between the two camps—dark, dreadful and meaningless to some, but light, guiding, and full of the best lessons to others. Without a saving knowledge of God, without implicit confidence in His infinite wisdom and goodness and love, without faith in Christ and trust in the precious promises of the gospel, one is all afloat on a stormy sea, under darkened heavens, in a rudderless vessel, and drifting he knows not whither. Disappointments come, and there is no compensation. The bleeding, sorrowing heart finds no healing, soothing balm. Losses and bereavements bring no fresh, rich, sweet experiences of Divine grace and love. The soul is in a cheerless solitude and a desert waste, its life-plans in disorder, its hopes wrecked, and breathing out on listless air its vain regrets and unanswerd questionings. Oh, if you have pity to feel and bestow, think of those in deep affliction and trial, who have no Father, no Saviour, no heavenly Comforter, no blessed and everlasting Refuge and promises, to fly to, and cling to, and rest in! They are in the Red Sea with the Egyptians. Others, who have these supports, may be in the same sea, but the cloudy Pillar is light to them, and the shore and the song are before them!

To the trusting beliver, how clear or certain is the ruling hand in each event of life! All intricate vicissitudes are plain to the eye of God. All tangled allotments fulfill His purpose; and all things, however unlikely in our view, work together for good to them that love Him. You go into a mechanic's shop, and see various sorts of tools; some have crooks, hooks or angles; others are of different shapes. You do not condemn these instruments because they do not all look handsome or straight. The mechanic makes use of them all in doing his work. So with God's providences; they may sometimes seem to us crooked and strange, yet they all carry on His work. I remember seeing in Paris some fine Gobelin tapestry, with history and pictures wrought into it with wonderful symmetry and beauty. Look at the wrong side of it, and you see threads, patches and dim outlines all in confusion. So with many providences; we can make nothing out of them from the wrong side; but look from the side where God looks upon them and brings them out in the warp and woof of His work and wisdom, and what admirable order and wonderful tracings of Divine and loving skill!

IV. LIFE'S PURPOSE OR END. It is seen or overlooked according as we place ourselves with reference to God's revelation. Many seem to live with no higher purpose than this world can give. Witness their pursuits, their plans, the ends they propose to themselves, and what inference would you draw? What would be the significance of these various lives? Would it not be severally, "How much of this world can I gain? What positions can I reach? What pleasures can I secure? What self-gratifications? What social enjoyments? What mental treasures? Or what can I do for those I love?" Every wish, every hope is bounded by an earthly horizon.

But those upon whom God's light and guidance shine, who look at this life in its true significance, have a higher purpose and a nobler end. There is something beyond the present passage. There is a celestial landing and a song of victory. Beyond this exodus and its boundary river, there is a land of promise and plenty, of beauty and glory. There is here a God to be recognized, loved and served; there is a Saviour who died for us, a redemption to be secured; a soul to be saved, an everlasting life in reserve; and this present state is the preparation-period. This life is a school for heaven. It has a nobler, grander purpose than earth or self. How shall I reach a glorious immortality? How can I save others, or so influence them that they shall not fail of life's true and blessed purpose? I put myself on the side of God, and in the light and guidance of His Pillar of Cloud and Fire. There only am I safe, and in the best sense useful.

V. Death and Eternity. Look at them from these opposite points. Are they not cloud and darkness to the unbeliever? Is there any relief from their Cimmerian gloom? any star of hope in that night? any joyous prospect beyond the shadowy valley? Is the traveler cheerful and happy as he approaches the boundary-line? Does the spirit plume its wings for an eagle-flight to the realm of eternal summer and sunshine with God and the holy of all ages? or does it sink in death and darkness, shattered and destroyed, like an old hulk after its last voyage? What is the testimony? Rev. Dr. Gardiner Spring says: "I have seen universalists and infidels die, and during a ministry of fifty-five years, I have not found a single instance of peace and joy in their views of eternity. No, nothing but an accusing conscience and the terrors of apprehension. I have seen men die who were men of mercurial temperament, men of pleasure and fun, men of taste and literature, lovers of the opera and the theater rather than the house of God; and I never saw an instance in which such men died in peace. They died as they lived. Life was a blank and death the king of terrors; a wasted life, an undone eternity."

While all is shadow and gloom, reluctance and terror, to the unbeliever, in view of his departure to the world of spirits and the presence of God; to the Christian, there is the light of hope, the peace of trust, the joyous sense of a present Saviour, the sweet song of victory, the bright prospect of a heavenly home. John Foster, in writing to a friend, said: "I congratulate you and myself that life is passing fast away. What a superlatively grand and consoling idea is that of death! Without this radiant idea, this delightful morning star, indicating that the luminary of eternity is going to rise, life would, in my view, darken into midnight melancholy. Thanks to that fatal decree that dooms us to die! thanks to that gospel which opens the vision of an endless life! and thanks above all to that Saviour friend who has promised to conduct all the faithful through the sacred trance of death, into scenes of Paradise and everlasting delight." Not only to the aged but to the youthful Christian as well, death is disarmed and the bright world beyond has wonderful attractions. In one of our New England villages a little boy was lying upon his death-bed, when suddenly raising himself he exclaimed, "Mother, mother! I see such a beautiful country, and so many little children who are beckoning me to them; but there are high mountains between us—too high for me to climb; who will carry me over?" He leaned back upon his pillow apparently in deep thought; when once more he partially rose, and stretching forth his little hands, he cried as loud as his feeble voice would permit, " Mother, mother! the Strong Man's come to carry me over the mountains:" then fell peacefully asleep, to awake in the beautiful land that dawned upon his vision. We have seen some of our dear ones die in the faith —in the love and peace of Jesus; and we could not but feel that what was an event of inexpressible sorrow to us, was to them an introduction to joys that are unspeakable and full of glory. Ours is the weight of bereavement, trial, toil, and grief; but theirs the raptures of heavenly bliss. Ours, the conflicts and weariness of this mortal state; theirs, the song of victory and the crown of glory.

The experience of God's people in every age confirms the truth of His word in regard to the rest and the blessedness that await them in their Father's house above. The experience of the unbelieving in view of their departure from earth into eternity also verifies the oft-repeated declaration of the Bible that neither light nor hope cheer their way to outer and eternal gloom. There are two camps as of old. On the one side there are light and guidance, victory and the better land; and on the other side cloud and darkness, defeat and death. Brethren, what encouragement you have to gird yourselves for the work and warfare of the Christian life, in view of the promised and rich reward! Oh friends, not yet enlisted with the Chosen People, when will you so learn this great lesson of the ages and of to-day, as to make it a matter of instant practical and momentous interest to yourselves? Has not the hour come for you to leave the enemy's camp, over which hangs impending doom, and by repentance of sin, and faith in our Lord Jesus Christ, place yourselves among the friends and servants of God? The gospel calls. The Saviour invites. The Spirit and the bride say, Come. Light shines from the guiding Pillar. How blessed the march to Canaan! How glorious the song, how fair the landscape, how sweet the springs, how rich the fruits and clusters on the other side of Jordan!

THE PILLAR OF CLOUD AND FIRE.

That mysterious column! it hung from the sky!
　The vanguard as Israel their exodus made;
'Twas a wonderful thing to each upward turned eye—
　A presence divine—the Shekinah displayed!

As it moved in its grandeur, their course was discerned;
　Its shadow, refreshing, soft over them lay;
How resplendent its form as to crimson it turned,
　And night wore a beauty unknown to the day!

In the midst of the Sea—its dark waters rolled back—
　The chosen go forward, walled billows between!
For they find in the depths solid ground for a track,—
　The marvelous Cloud brooding over the scene!

All defiant, the foe presses on in their path;
　The Pillar, receding, the armies divides;
To Egyptian pursuers 'tis darkness and wrath;
　On Israel's camp its bright glory abides!

Full enswathed in its radiance, the passage complete,
   They, grateful and safe on the welcoming shore,
Lift their song to Jehovah—its chorus repeat—
   An anthem of triumph that rings evermore!

To the long journey's end, as the chosen of God
   To desert or mountain or river-bank came,
In the places of rest, in the pathways they trod,
   Their guide was the Pillar of Cloud and of Flame.

When the night-gloom was deepest, to them it gave light;
   To nations opposed, it was darkness severe:
So the light of God shines on the pure in his sight,
   While souls without faith grope in shadow and fear.

WEST SIDE OF ST GILES'S.

SERMON VIII.

THE CALL AND THE RESPONSE.

———

Atlantic Ocean.

PREFATORY NOTES.

DURING my second tour in Europe, I had the pleasant company, much of the time, of Rev. Dr. S. Graves of Grand Rapids, Mich., Dr. E. M. Snow of Providence, R. I., and the late Gen. A. Pilsbury of Albany, N. Y. The tour embraced a trip in Scotland from Edinburgh to Glasgow, Ayr, and northward along the Crinin and Caledonian canals to Inverness, and back by railway through the Highlands to Edinburgh. Thence we went to London, stopping at Melrose and York. We attended as delegates, the International Prison Congress in London, July, 1872, where we met several distinguished persons from different parts of Europe, among them Sir John Bowring, Cardinal Manning, Earl of Carnavon, and Prince of Wales. While there we heard Rev. Mr. Spurgeon and Dr. W. Landels, and had pleasant interviews with them. Afterward we went to Paris, Geneva, Berne, and other Swiss towns, and spent some days in traversing passes and climbing famous Alpine mountains, returning by Basle to Paris, London and Edinburgh.

With my dear friends, the Douglases, I passed several delightful days, and then went to Liverpool, having secured a passage on the fine White Star Steamship Adriatic. On going to my state-room, I was glad to find as its other occupants Rev. Dr. Philip Schaff, and a Yale student. It was also pleasant to find several who were fellow-voyagers on the outward passage, and some others whom I knew. This homeward trip was every way delightful. The weather was fine, the sea generally calm, and the passengers social and agreeable—among whom were Ex-Gov. Holley of Connecticut, Judge Ward Hunt of New York, and lawyer Shearman of Brooklyn. We had several good entertainments, as lectures, poems, concerts, etc. We had two services on Sunday. On invitation I preached in the morning the following sermon, Dr. Schaff reading the hymns, and Capt. Murray the church service. In the evening Dr. Schaff preached from John iii. 16.

At the close of one of our pleasant evening entertainments, I read the following impromptu verses which seemed to give pleasure, and numerous copies of them were solicited.

> While now we have passed o'er the line of mid-ocean,
>   And grandly sweep on through the foam,
> How sweet is each thought, with its tender emotion,
>   Of loved ones we long for at home!
>
> And when they are filled, these dear hopes so ecstatic,
>   We'll think of the voyage we have past;
> O the bright happy days on the proud Adriatic
>   Shall ever in memory last.
>
> These scenes and these friendships, thro' life's din and hurry,
>   Shall linger as treasures of mind;
> For surely we'll cherish our good Captain MURRAY,
>   And officers genial and kind.
>
> And those who have sung for us, those who have spoken,
>   Words, music enchantingly sweet,
> Shall all be remembered while years are unbroken,
>   And hearts with affection shall beat.

THE CALL AND THE RESPONSE.

Preached on the White-Star Steamship Adriatic,
on the Homeward Atlantic Voyage,
Lord's Day, Sept. 1, 1872.

Psalm xlii. 7.—DEEP CALLETH UNTO DEEP.

IT is not the literal sea, storm-tossed, rolling, roaring, breaking, under clouds of darkness, that is in the Psalmist's mind, save as an illustration of the swelling emotions of the human heart stirred to its mighty depths. There are times when such a billowy sea and frowning sky are the fit emblem of the smitten or troubled soul. Yet from the searchless recesses within, the anxious spirit sends its cry into the dark and awful deep above. For Jehovah is there. His judgments are a great deep. He is a God that hideth Himself. Darkness is His secret place; His pavilion round about Him dark waters, and thick clouds of the skies. So to His dear servant David, God sometimes appeared; and the burdened soul, from the abyss of its quenchless desires, sent up its longings, aspirations and prayers to the infinite depths of the Divine nature, power and dispensations. In his absence from the house of prayer, the Psalmist's heart panted, thirsted for God. "Why art thou cast down, oh my soul? and why art thou disquieted within me? Hope thou in God; for I shall yet praise Him for the help of His countenance. Oh my God, my soul is cast down within me: therefore will I remember thee from the land of Jordan, and of the Hermonites, from the hill Mizar. Deep calleth unto deep at the noise of thy waterspouts: all thy waves and thy billows are gone over me."

There are no deeps in this world so vast, so profound, so unfathomable, as those of the human soul. The Mediterranean Sea, whence David drew the figure of the text, has been sounded, and a cable stretched along its deep bed, amid wrecks and pearls, as a channel for human thoughts. Men have dug far into the earth in their search for treasures. But who has found the lowest stratum of thought or feeling or capacity of the human spirit? Ah, there are deeps *there* unknown even to its possessor. And *there* are wrecks and pearls, too, along which go thoughts, struggling, swelling, aspiring, and calling, in a felt weakness, dependence and need, to "the deep things of God." And how profoundly and infinitely deep the Divine nature, attributes and purposes! "Who by searching can find out the Almighty?" No words can express the vastness of this idea, the depths of God's being, God's thoughts, God's designs. But the deep in man may and does call to the deep in God. Our human nature has a powerful yearning for the Divine. The filial, loving soul says:

> "My God, my life, my love,
> To thee, to thee I call:
> I cannot live, if thou remove,
> For thou art all in all."

And to such a soul, to every soul that truly, sincerely calls, there is a gracious response, a blessed answer. It does not call in vain. Out of that great upper deep comes a voice to cheer, and a hand to help. What are some of those conditions and circumstances of life, when the text fits into our own experience—when the soul longs, aspires, cries for light, help and life in God?

One of these conditions and experiences is, I apprehend, when there first comes to the mind, *a deep sense or consciousness of alienation from God.* The soul begins to perceive its own disquietude and unrest; its condition of spiritual orphanage, and separation from its heavenly

Father. Along with this feeling there is the yearning desire, though it may not be expressed, to have this barrier to holy and peaceful fellowship with God removed. Emotions, thoughts, longings are kindled and active down in the depths of the immortal spirit. There they linger, now apparently slumbering, and now powerfully energetic, almost irrepressible, in their strong and earnest wish for something that only God can give. Oh that there might be a realization of that of which the need is so deeply felt!

How early in life these emotions, so profound, so sacred, so solemn, exist and are cherished. They live in the young mind. They dwell there like influences, like persuasive voices, from other worlds, like seeds of eternity springing up and growing in our spiritual nature, permeating and energizing all its powers. Go back to your childhood, and think over its thoughts, recall its memories, cherish again its emotions and aspirings, and you will find this confirmed in your own experience. There are great deeps even in a a child's soul, where solemn thoughts and images of God spring; where vivid ideas of spiritual things, eternal realities, and future existences abound; and where there are unutterable longings and desires toward the Infinite. The very crude, indistinct and even erroneous conceptions of these things, often show how real, how strong, and how influential they are. If the experience of our childhood in regard to God, to sin, to death, to heaven and hell, were written out, how curious, how interesting, how instructive the chapters of that history would be! Those early prayers and desires would show the deeps of the soul calling to the deeps of the Divine Being. What *we* felt and now dimly remember, others are feeling to-day. Let these dear children tell us what they think, how they feel, how they pray at times, and what their longings sometimes are towards God and heaven, and we should find wondrous things hidden in the depths of their hearts. But they never do, they never will, they never can tell half of their experience in these things. We sometimes overhear their conversations about them. Not a few have felt as did the Prodigal Son, a sense of loss and deprivation, a beginning to be in want, a desire to go to their Father's house. Ah! these youth and children, that boy and girl, have reflected and wept, it may be, and prayed and longed to make known their thoughts and desires, but could not, dared not, except it were perhaps in solitude to God. Oh there are in the silent depths of the young soul, callings, utterances, inaudible and noiseless, yet real and strong, rising up toward the infinite.

It is childhood, weak and helpless, under its early consciousness of alienation, crying for its Father and God.

There is a difference in respect to these calls, wide and marked. Some are the expressions of true prayer from penitent believing hearts. Such souls realize what they ask and long for. They come to God. They give themselves up to the lead and love of Jesus, and so become true children of their Heavenly Father. Their prayers are heard and answered, and so they come into the household of God and are at rest and happy.

Others call, but it is only the overflow of their emotions, the expression of their sympathetic natures—prayers, desires, that do not go from earnest, persistent, trusting hearts, with a giving up of the world and a sweet loving faith in Christ. Longings for the better good are not followed out. There is a *call* to God, but not a *going* to Him. The deeps in the soul cry out in their imperfect sense of want; but there is not a readiness to have God come and fill those deeps with His presence and grace. No—there is a stronger desire for the world to come in and take possession. Has not this been the experience of some of you?

Another condition where the text fits into human feeling is that of *powerful conviction of sin*. Then the overwhelmed and sinking spirit out of its depths calls upon God for help and deliverance. From the verge of despair and ruin, guilty, condemned and perishing, it cries in its extremity and as its last hope for mercy, to Christ the only Saviour. Oh what a call, what a prayer is that, what an earnest, agonizing, outgoing and uplifting of the poor, broken, humbled heart, when it casts itself as a helpless, worthless thing into the arms of bleeding mercy! What crying supplication is that, when a sin-burdened soul comes to the foot of the cross and says, " Lord, save, or I perish." It is deep calling unto deep. Many do not find out till such a time what depths of sin their hearts contained. The heavens frowning, the billows of conviction rolling as if to engulf them, they perceive the truth of God's word by the prophet: " The wicked are like the troubled sea, when it cannot rest, whose waters cast up mire and dirt." A life in opposition to the will of God; trampling upon His unfailing mercies; forgetful of His constant goodness; rejecting His most reasonable claims; disregarding His holy Word, breaking His law and spurning His gospel; turning away from the Person and pleadings of His Son; repeatedly grieving His Holy Spirit;

slighting opportunities given in forbearing love; remaining unmoved under the messages, warnings and prayers of His servants. Oh, when all this is seen in light from eternity, disclosing the infinite holiness of God, how does the soul sink under its many and aggravated offences! What ingratitude! what thoughtless heaven-daring folly and presumption! The sinner looks into the deeps of his wicked, miserable heart, and sees himself a subject of God's righeous wrath, and only fit for it, as he stands on the verge of perdition. The depths of hell are calling for him, and seem opening to receive him. But he can not escape. He has exhausted all his resources. He can work out no righteousness to satisfy his conscience, or to robe him for the presence of God. No safety, no release, no peace comes. He is as one wrecked in the sea, and sinking in the yawning billows. But, in his extremity, he cries to the only source of help. Ah! it is *that* cry, that deep calling unto deep, a voice of prayer and faith from the depths of a sinful soul, reaching the depths of mercy and salvation in Christ that avails and brings relief. Then the stormy agitation ceases and Jesus says to the winds and waves, Be still! Oh what a blessed response to the soul from the depths of infinite mercy and grace! To know that there is a mighty Saviour in such an hour; to be able to call upon Him and realize His aid; to have Him come and deliver, and forgive, and bestow His love and comfort—is there any blessing that can compare with it? How many poor, perishing souls at such an hour have found Him just such a matchless Friend—have called to Him, and the saving response has come. How many, since the publican cried for mercy; since the leper's prayer was answered, "I will, be thou clean;" since blind Bartimeus effectually called; since the Syrophœnician woman said, "Help me;" since the thousands at the day of Pentecost cried out in the conviction of sin, and were directed to Christ; since Saul of Tarsus, prostrate at the feet of Jesus prayed, "Lord, what wilt thou have me to do?"—since the Philippian jailer cried, "What must I do to be saved?"—how many have heard the blessed response of redeeming mercy! Oh, if there were no Saviour in those great deeps of God above, to whom our soul-depth calls, how unavailing would be our cries, how hopeless our doom! Happy is he who calls and calls till the gracious response of pardon and peace comes. Some there are even under pungent conviction of sin who, not calling upon and yielding to Christ, call to other things— deeps of sinful pleasure, of dark unbelief, of dread waters that drown men's souls in perdition.

Another condition in which the text fits our experience is that of *bereavement and trial.* The tempted, struggling and sorrowing soul, in its deep fears and heaving emotions, agitated and anxious, cries out to God, to lift off the burden, to roll back the overwhelming waves, to assuage the swelling griefs, or impart strength and grace to the sinking, troubled heart. The Psalmist had sore afflictions. Great trials weighed down his spirit. But in them all, and far away from the house and people of God, he did not forget his almighty Refuge. He turned his thoughts toward Him whose judgments are a great deep, and who does not willingly afflict nor grieve the children of men; who had sustained and comforted him in the past, and whose unchanging love and protection he could still share. The troubled deeps of his soul cried out in confidence and hope to Him, in whom he knew there were depths of mercy and consolation that no human want could exhaust. Ah! those terrible bereavements that sometimes come to us, how even for a long time after they occur the effect now and then is like a great overwhelming wave that seems to bury us under its dark oppressive flood. Our very selves have gone into the grave with those we loved. And if it were not for Jesus walking upon the sea, and coming to us through the darkness with

His soothing voice of peace and comfort, what could we do? God's children have often been afflicted. What persecutions, losses, conflicts, trials some of them have suffered for the name of Christ. What disappointments, heart-sorrows, unknown to the world, strivings against the ills of life, heavy burdens of their lot with little of human help and sympathy. They adopt the words of the Psalmist, "Out of the depths have I cried unto thee, O Lord." But in all this how have their souls gone out in supplication and longing to God, in tender and loving sympathy with Christ, whose woes and griefs were greater than ours, and whose consolations and supports are most ample for all our need. Deep calleth unto deep; nor is the call in vain. The tempted find strength. The afflicted are solaced. The mourners are comforted. The weak are made strong. The desponding begin to rejoice. See Jacob prevailing at Peniel; Moses as he prayed between the living and the dead, intercepting the thunderbolts of wrath; Job in a sublime patience that brought its reward; Elijah and Daniel answered in miracles; our Lord Himself in the garden, and Satan vanquished; the church in supplication and Peter delivered; and Paul and Silas in midnight prayer set free. The martyrs have cried, How long, O Lord! and not in vain; parents for erring children; churches for revivals; servants of God suffering cruel injustice—Bunyan in jail; Judson in prison—Oh how many in the depths of their souls have appealed to the depths of the Divine mercy and power, and found deliverance or all-sufficient grace.

> "What though the *floods* lift up their voice,
> Thou hearest, Lord *our* louder cry;
> They can not damp thy children's joys,
> Or shake the soul when God is nigh."

There is another condition and extremity—*the dying hour*—when deep calleth unto deep; when the *trusting* soul lifts up its desires and hopes confidently to God through the grace of Christ. Then is the conflict with the last enemy. Then the soul stands on the confines both of earth and heaven. Then the believer commits himself to the swellings of Jordan. Solemn hour! when weakness hangs on immortal strength; when death looks longingly to life; when the Christian triumphs in his departure, and the savor of victory and immortality hallows the sacred calm of the last sleep. Say, is not our holy faith a glorious thing, as it enables us to look from the deep valley of the shadow of death with serene confidence to the light and glory of the eternal hills! from the crumbling tabernacle of this earthly house to the building of God, the house not made with hands! from the dark billows to the shining shore! So Stephen, with a vision of heaven opened, called upon God, saying, Lord Jesus, receive my spirit. So the great Apostle looked away into the deep realities and rewards of eternity, and cheerfully, hopefully and happily resigned this life and world, saying, I am now ready to be offered—I have fought a good fight, 1 have finished my course, I have kept the faith; and he knew the righteous Judge would give him the crown.

I might give instances, more than you have time to hear, of departing saintly souls calling to the depth of eternity, and finding it not dark and dread, but beautiful and radiant. Said one, "Glory to God! I see heaven sweetly opened before me!" Said another: "Oh, how this soul of mine longs to be gone, like a bird out of his cage, to the realms of bliss." Dr. Judson once said, "I am not tired of my work, neither am I tired of the world; yet when Christ calls me home, I shall go with the gladness of a boy bounding away from school." Said Mrs. Hemans, the poetess, "I feel as if I were sitting with Mary at the feet of my Redeemer, hearing the music of His voice." Lady Huntingdon said, "I shall go to my Father this night." And the dying injunction of the mother of the Wesleys was, "Children, when I am gone, sing a song of praise to God." So the followers of Christ leave these earthly scenes, with the glory of the summer land of song in view, calling, longing for the fathomless depths of the blessedness of heaven. And how sweetly the voices from those upper deeps summon the Christian to his rest: "Child, your Father calls, come home." As the shadows of evening fall, we stand in the door of our dwelling, and call for our children in the street to come into the house. We want them with us. So our Father stands at the door of heaven, and looks with loving eye upon His children in the paths of their pilgrimage on earth, and He says to them at the evening of life, "Come up higher!" and all the family shall be there at length. God grant that we, fellow-voyagers together now, may all at last reach that heavenly home!

A MEMORIAL.

*When thou passest through the waters I will be with thee;
and through the rivers, they shall not overflow thee.*
ISAIAH XLIII. 2.

DEEP calleth unto deep! The sky seems falling,
    Whelmed in wild sea and cloud;
And o'er the waste a sunset gloom appalling
    Shuts like an iron shroud.

Saviour! till on the waves thy form beholding,
    Our hearts find no release;
Come through the darkness all the world enfolding,
    And speak to us thy peace.

Life's brightest hope, the gift most fondly cherished,
    Home's fairest, loveliest light,
All, in this great bereavement, faded, perished—
    Day darkened into night.

Didst thou, in hidden love, oh pitying Father!
    Make in our hearts this dearth?
Or, for the happier home in glory rather,
    Long for thy child on earth?

Her life was beautiful in rich completenes,
    Beyond her years so fair ;
For heaven's pure dawning such a radiant meetness,
    Like a full morning star.

Her mind was peerless in its ample treasure
    Of varied gifts and grace :
Wide fields of culture, with a lofty pleasure,
    'Twas hers with ease to trace.

Wrapt in the tender folds of our affection,
    Her smile as sunlight fair,
Her words, her presence, like heaven's sweet reflection;
    Can we the jewel spare ?

By weeks of weariness and pain consuming,
    Pressed to the verge of life,
Her trusting spirit, with an angel's pluming,
    Soared from the tranquil strife.

The next grand moment, as at once awaking
    From wondrous dreaming strange,
Within the gates, her raptured view is taking
    The City's glorious range.

O, the sweet thrill of that survey celestial,
    The blessed CHRIST to see !
With dear ones, known and loved in years terrestrial,
    Again with joy to be !

WHITE STAR STEAMER ADRIATIC.

SERMON IX.

CHRIST'S WORK FOR THE HUMAN RACE.

At Sea, Off the West Coast of Ireland.

PREFATORY NOTES.

A THIRD trip to Europe before the issue of this book allows the addition to it of another sermon preached abroad. This time my dear wife shared and enjoyed the journey with me. We left New York for Glasgow, July 14, 1881, on the steamship State of Indiana. We had for the most part fine weather and a very pleasant company of passengers, among them ten clergymen and several physicians. The voyage included two Sabbaths; and though invited to preach on the first, I prefered to hear one of the several Methodist ministers on board. Rev. B. St. James Fry, D. D., of St. Louis preached. On the second Sabbath came the sermon here given while we were off the west coast of Ireland. Rev. S. D. McConnell of Middletown, Conn., read the English Church Service, and the hymns, "Rock of Ages, cleft for me," and "Jesus, Lover of my soul," were sung.

The next day we landed, and after looking about Glasgow went to Edinburgh and were heartily welcomed by our dear friends, Mr. T. G Douglas and family, whose many kindnesses we shall always remember. We made various excursions, including trips to Lochs Katrine and Lomond, and to Melrose, Abbotsford and Dryburgh Abbey. We then went to London, stopping by the way at Leeds, York, Sheffield, Kettering and Bedford. At Mr. Burr's in London we found Mr. James Hay, Jr., wife and sister, of Woodstock, Ontario, delightful fellow-voyagers on the Atlantic, and with them we visited places of interest in the city and vicinity and also went to Paris and Switzerland. Returning to Edinburgh, we passed more pleasant days with our friends, and visited with Mr. and Mrs. Douglas dear Deacon Hugh Rose and daughter at their summer abode in Callender.

On two Sundays in London we heard Mr. Spurgeon at his Tabernacle, and after one of these memorable services we had a precious interview with the great preacher. In Paris we had the pleasure of hearing a sermon from Bishop M. Simpson of Philadelphia. In Edinburgh we attended a service at Dr. Horatius Bonar's church, and had a few pleasant words with him ; heard Rev. Mr. Muir, pastor of the Established Presbyterian church at Morningside, and I preached for him on a Sabbath in his absence. We saw a son and daughter of Queen Victoria —the Duke of Edinburgh at Leith, and the Marchioness of Lorne at our hotel in Berne.

Taking leave of our beloved friends, Sept. 16th, we proceeded to Glasgow and embarked at evening on the State of Indiana. The next day we had a few hours at Larne, Ireland, giving us time to visit the village on a jaunting car. We were glad to find several of our outward-bound passenger-friends taking the homeward voyage with us. On the first Sabbath I preached at the request of Capt. Saddler. This passage was long and exceedingly rough and tempestuous, some days the waves rolling "mountains high." The last evening on the steamship we had a pleasant literary entertainment. The first news, obtained from a pilot boat as we approached New York harbor, was the death of the lamented President Garfield.

CHRIST'S WORK FOR THE HUMAN RACE.

Preached on the Steamship State of Indiana, on the Passage from New York to Glasgow, Sunday, July 24, 1881.

John i. 9.—THAT WAS THE TRUE LIGHT, WHICH LIGHTETH EVERY MAN THAT COMETH INTO THE WORLD.

BOLD and broad is this declaration, and yet there are a number of other passages of similar import. Let me call your attention to them, and to the important truths that underlie them and constitute their real meaning. The passages are those that connect our Lord's life and work with the whole human race. I here name some of them. In announcing the Saviour's birth at Bethlehem, the angel said to the shepherds, "Behold, I bring you good tidings of great joy, which shall be *to all people.*" When Jesus came to the Jordan to be baptized of John, the latter exclaimed, "Behold the Lamb of God which taketh away *the sin of the world.*" In the night interview with Nicodemus, our Lord said, "God so loved *the world* that He gave His only begotten Son ;" and again, " that *the world through Him might be saved.*" In the sixth chapter He said: " I am the living bread which came down from heaven ; if any man eat of this bread he shall live forever ; and the bread that I will give is my flesh, which I will give *for the life of the world.*" In chapter xii., referring to His death on the cross, He said: "And I, if I be lifted up from the earth, *will draw all men unto me.*"

These are passages from the Gospels. We find similar ones in the Epistles. In Romans v. Paul says : "As by the offence of one judgment came upon all men to condemnation, even so by the righteousness of One the free gift *came upon all men* unto justification of life." In 1 Timothy we have the passages : "We trust in the living God, who is *the Saviour of all men*, especially of those that believe ;" and, "who will have *all men to be saved* and to come unto the knowledge of the truth." In Hebrews ii. it is written : " We see Jesus, who was made a little lower than the angels for the suffering of death, crowned with glory and honor, that He by the grace of God should *taste death for every man.*" In 1 John ii. we find: " He is the propitiation for our sins ; and not for ours only, but also for *the sins of the whole world.*"

These passages surely teach us that Christ sustains a peculiar relation to the whole human race.

He has done something in His life and death for the benefit of all. He lightens every man that comes into the world. By God's grace His death touched every case; and in some sense He takes away the world's sin. Men are in a different relation to God—on a better footing than they would have been if Christ had not come. What are these advantages? How is every person as it were changed in his relations by what Christ has done and suffered? This is what I shall attempt to show.

But allow me to say, in passing, that these passages do *not* properly teach that all men will be saved. Some, anxious to make out such a doctrine from the Scriptures, have put this construction upon them. But they will not bear it. Other passages with which they stand, forbid this meaning. The general, obvious tenor of the Bible is against it. Its teaching is so clear and impressive in respect to the future life and rewards, that the few passages I have quoted, while they overflow with the Divine benevolence and love, and show that the scheme of redemption affects the relations of the whole race, yet they do not assure us that all men will be saved. The Scriptures every where speak of conditions of salvation. There must be regeneration, faith, repentance, holy living, love to God, obedience to Christ.

Character, meetness for Heaven must come into the account. The Bible speaks of some that are lost eternally, that never obtain forgiveness, for whom it would be better not to have been born, that shall not inherit the kingdom of heaven. So there may be a Saviour for all people, an influence from Christ and His death that shall reach all, every man, and God in His infinite love may desire all men to be saved and to come to the knowledge of the truth; and yet some may fail of eternal life by failing to meet the conditions of salvation. The state, the city, the town, may provide educational advantages for every child, every youth, and still some may neglect them and grow up ignorant. A kind father may do every thing needful and more for the welfare of his children; but some of them may not appreciate his kindness, and so fail of its benefits.

One way in which an influence from Christ reaches every person in the world, is that of securing for each a PROBATION or day of grace. The first sin deserved condign punishment. If full justice had been meeted out at once, the race would have been swept out of existence, or left hopeless on the face of the earth. In the day of their transgression they would have perished. So "God spared not the *angels* that sinned, but cast them down to hell." With the human race God chose to deal differently. He had devised a plan of redemption. This gracious economy required a probation. Under it, sentence against an evil work is not speedily executed. There is divine forbearance, patience, long-suffering. But this is all in consequence of the mediatorial work of Christ. So far He takes away the sin of the world, or delays the consequences of sin, that all men may have a space for repentance. Christ has given His life for the world in that the world is spared from immediate destruction. Men live, each has his period of probation on earth, because Christ has lived here. He stands between God and the speedy execution of justice upon the guilty, as Moses stood between the living and the dead and stayed the plague. Let every per-on know that he lives, goes about his business, has his allotted time on earth; and so all the complicated affairs of this great world go on, and men develop their characters as they will or please, because we live under a redemptive economy through Christ. Do not forget, my friends, that you owe your very life to Christ. Each day, every opportunity is a gift from Him. He is the natural and intellectual and probational light of every man that cometh into the world.

In this view, again, Christ benefits the entire race, inasmuch as all our TEMPORAL BLESSINGS are the result of His mediation. All over the wide world whatever is fitted to augment human comfort and happiness; whatever delights the eye, rejoices the mind, enraptures the heart, or innocently gratifies the senses, ennobles the faculties, and makes life a possession to be desired and enjoyed—all this comes to us and to all men through the Son of God. He procured them by His mediation. He purchased them by His life. As a king scatters gifts among the people on the way to his coronation and throne, so Christ, in His triumphal march from the first promise of a Saviour to the final consummation of his gracious kingdom, through symbol and prophecy and actual advent and intercession, scatters among men in all the human generations, every temporal blessing they enjoy. From hence is every good and perfect gift. Forget not, O friend, that every thing valuable, every thing precious, every thing dear to you in this world, with all the possibilities of existence here, was procured for you by the Lord Jesus Christ, your and the world's Redeemer.

Again, Christ, by what He has done, sets the whole race of man in A NEW AND FAVORABLE ATTITUDE TOWARDS GOD. He lifts them up from the hopelessness of the Fall. He breaks the deep night of despair. He flings a heavenly radiance into the very darkness of death. He takes all men out of the prison-house of doom, and sets them on the vantage-ground of a new trial full of hope and life. So He lifts up our fallen race, and draws all men toward Himself. So far the propitiation of the cross was a propitiation for the sins of the whole world. In the conflict of Gethsemane there might be a victory for every man. In the death-pang of Calvary there might be a life-warrant for every condemned soul. The crimson stream from the cross might purify every sin-defiled heart. "It is finished" was the announcement of a redemption sufficient for every case. So far does the Lamb of God take away the *sin of the world.* The iron grasp of sin is broken. It is no longer necessarily fatal. This appalling aspect of it is taken away. Death is tasted for every man in the cup of Golgotha. Salvation is free for the world. The Jew and the Gentile are welcome. The civilized and the barbarian, the Parthian and the Scythian, the learned and the ignorant—the high up and the low down in the human scale—whosoever will, let him come and partake freely. God is no respecter of persons; but in every nation he that fears Him and works righteousness is accepted of Him.

It is a grand thought, Christ giving Himself, His life for the world, and so lifting up every man of our race from a hopeless, helpless state, and bringing him within reach of eternal life. To what high privileges it introduces us! What matchless possibilities it places before us! That Child in the manger of Bethlehem was set for the rising of many. What a hold upon our wrecked humanity Christ got when He took our nature, when God was manifest in the flesh, when He came down to every man's lowest condition. The poor, blind and wretched heathen, if he but thought of God and saw Him in the sun, the stars, the forest or the flower, and felt his own sinfulness, and longed for pardon, and wondered if his soul might rest in some pure and happy home with God—if there were in him a disposition to live up to the light already given, and to receive the Christ that might be revealed—such an one, no doubt, in virtue of the atonement would be saved. Many such we believe are saved. And the most enlightened soul must accept the same Saviour in the Gospel, if he would enter heaven. The little child just thinking and reading of Jesus can be gathered in the arms of the Good Shepherd; and the strong man and veteran, to be saved, must find shelter in the same bosom of Infinite Love. O how near to Himself the lifted-up Christ has drawn all men! He has brought them over what were otherwise a bridgeless gulf. He has taken them from a region of utter despair and set them in the border-land of hope and life. He has laid hold of the wrecked and stranded vessel of humanity and lifted it upon a fairer sea and near a heavenly port.

Another illustration of the way in which the work of Christ is a benefit to the entire human race, is its application to the SALVATION OF INFANTS. We believe that all little children are saved who die before arriving to years of accountability. They have not committed actual sin, nor incurred personal guilt. Offspring of a sinful race, they are yet safe within the folds and arms of Christ's sacrificial work. They are reached by that great and gracious provision. The Bible says but little on the subject—its truths are addressed to responsible agents—but what it does say accords with our faith in the Divine goodness and the glory of a redemption that secures the salvation of infants. Those little budding flowers, early fading from earth, are brightly blooming in heaven. David's prophecy, " I shall go to him," is realized in the salvation and re-union of parent and child. The Shunammite's confidence, "It is well," had in it heavenly hope. When Jesus said we must "be converted and become as little children," and "of such is the kingdom of heaven," our faith becomes assurance. Our little ones, no more with us, are with the Good Shepherd in Paradise. So *all* little children, in every age and place, thus early taken from earth—to the number of half the human race—are safe in heaven. And so all that live, while of such tender age, without idea of responsibility, are in a certain sense in a state of salvation. They are encompassed and embraced with the redeeming provisions of the Great Sacrifice. The whole race was involved in the catastrophe of Adam's sin. The whole race is benefited by the work of the second Adam. He throws His loving arms about every child, who is safe, till there is personal sin and guilt. In this delightful view God in Christ is the Saviour of all men. But when infancy is past, years of accountability reached, and sins are committed, then Christ is the actual Saviour only of those who believe. Faith is the prerequisite of salvation to all who are capable of believing. What an interesting thought that Christ has taken us all in His arms of redeeming love and mercy, as He literally took the little children that were brought to Him and blessed them with prayer and benediction. You can hardly think that one of those who felt the Holy Hands upon its head, who remembered the scene or was frequently reminded of it by the loving mother who witnessed it, would afterwards grow up to persist in sin and unbelief, an enemy of Christ and a rejecter of His salvation. Is not your guilt as great and your condemnation as fearful, if you refuse to believe in Jesus, if you prefer the world to Him, turning away from the Voice that speaks from heaven?

The cradle at Bethlehem somehow represented all other cradles. The Divine Infant there bore a peculiar relation to all other infants. The Holy Child Jesus, born of a human mother, in a sense sanctifies every birth, and is the Light that lighteth every man that cometh into the world. A higher value is given to the soul, a more precious interest clusters about it, from the fact of Christ's incarnation and the work He has wrought and the possibilities thus opened to all. The mother looks at her treasure in the cradle or the crib with a different feeling and a deeper hope, because the Son of God once lay in the manger. O, if Jesus thus went down to our lowest weakness and went up with us through every stage to manhood, that He might know every need, share every feeling, and meet every want, giving His life for the world, and drawing all men toward Himself; how great must be the guilt that breaks away from such a Saviour, that counts His sacrifice as worthless, and His salvation as inferior to the short-lived pleasures of sin. Lifted to such a height by the condescension of Christ, illumined by the light He imparts, your fall from thence, O unbeliever! must be deeper than that of the first sin, and your darkness more dread and hopeless than its despair!

There is one more way in which Christ brings light and hope to all the human race. It is in the PROVISION OF MERCY AND GRACE in the Gospel, so rich, full, and free. It was this glorious view of redemption that led the beloved disciple to say: "If any man sin, we have an Advocate with the Father, Jesus Christ the righteous; and He is the propitiation for our sins; and not for ours only, but also for the sins of the whole world." A propitiation is such an intervention or sacrifice by Christ as provides for the canceling of sin and the reconciliation of the believer to God. The work of Christ, His whole work, in the scheme of human redemption, was necessary to the salvation of a single soul. Not one of our race could be reached and ransomed, but for the incarnation, touch, and work of Christ—but for His life on earth; but for His sufferings in the garden; but for His death on the Cross; but for His resurrection, ascension, intercession and gift of the Holy Spirit. Think of the infinite outlay, that one lost sinner might be saved, that one poor child of Adam might be rescued from death eternal. Well may believers say, "We are bought with a price," and esteem the treasure of redeeming grace a "great salvation." Every sinner's pardon cost the blood of the Son of God. No name could be written in the Book of Life but by the Hand that was nailed to the cross. It is impossible to show the full measure of the sacrifice or work requisite for the salvation of one soul, yours or mine. If there had been but one to be saved, nothing less than "Christ and Him Crucified," with all the infinite meaning of that phrase, could save that one soul. But the means that saves one may save another. And as the resources of grace are as boundless as the attributes of God, there is no limit to the redemption of sinners, but their own determined and persistent refusal to repent and believe. Paul says that in his case the chief of sinners was saved. Therefore the most hardened and guilty everywhere *may* be saved. The propitiatory offering that has availed for so many, and for most desperate cases, is sufficient in its provisions of mercy for all, for the sins of the whole world. It is adapted to men everywhere, of all nations, conditions, peculiarities. There is not a sinner on the face of the earth, whose case may not be fully met in the riches of grace in Christ Jesus. We may single out any soul any where and tell him most earnestly and truthfully, that salvation is provided for him, that the death of Christ was for him, that the invitations of the Gospel are to him, that God is just as sincere in desiring his salvation, just as good and gracious in providing a Saviour for him, as if he were the only soul in the universe that needed to be saved —as if all the riches of redeeming love were for him alone!

You visit a building where there is an intricate and wonderful machine. It receives the rough, shapeless and soiled material, and delivers it in the form of a beautiful and useful fabric or utensil. You watch the operation. No matter how ugly, broken, shattered, ill-formed, or discolored the material, it comes out in every instance the shapely, fair, and beautiful object. Now the machine that can make one of these transformations, if its capacity were sufficient, and if it did not wear out by use, could in time exhaust all the material supplied. This is a poor illustration. It does not sufficiently show the adaptation of God's plan of mercy to meet every case in a world of sinners. There is no exhausting the treasures of Divine grace; no limiting the power of God in the Gospel; no measuring the extent of the atonement, or abridging the ability of Him who can save to the uttermost, and whose grace that bringeth salvation hath appeared to all men in its glorious amplitude and its wonderful adaptation.

The text, as thus opened, discloses to us the marvelous benevolence of God, the boundlessness of His love, the feelings of His infinitely compassionate heart toward men. God is love. He loves the world. He loves every soul of our sinful race. He longs for their salvation. He has made provision sufficient for every case. The costliest price He has paid. He would have all men to be saved. He is not willing that any should perish. And those who do perish, go down to death resisting His will, rejecting His salvation, refusing the riches of His grace, spurning His unspeakable gift, and trifling with His infinite love. He grieves over the course of such. His language is: " Hear, O heavens, and be astonished, O earth! for I have nourished and brought up children, and they have rebelled against me."

This theme furnishes what an encouragement to all who are laboring for the salvation of souls. What a Gospel we have to present to men—how ample, rich, complete! It is adapted to every person. With what confidence can its acceptance be urged! And what inspiring hope may well cheer the laborer!

Here, also, we recall the fact that salvation may be provided, and yet not be received. There may be, there is, a plenitude of grace and life, enough for every soul; and yet some may fail of the blessing. God sends His sunlight and rain upon the just and the unjust, but some neither sow nor reap. "To you is the word of this salvation sent," but some of you may not welcome it. God has given you the power of choice. You can accept or you can reject the heavenly gift. You can build on the Rock or the sand. O remember how essential it is that you *take* the water of life; that you *lay hold* on the hope set before you; that you *believe* on the Lord Jesus Christ. You must *choose the good part* or it never will be yours.

Think, finally, what it must be to neglect a salvation so great and free. The loss must be in proportion. How deep the darkness of that soul that refuses to be savingly illumined by the Light that lightens every man that cometh into the world!